LINCOLN CHRISTIAN U

W9-BUE-477

IN THE
SHADOW
OF THE
STEEPLE

"In the Shadow of the Steeple is Gene Williams's gift to the pastors and laity in America's smaller churches. Too many are discouraged in a church world with seemingly only one question, 'How many did you have Sunday?' He writes wisely as one who has pastored small, middle, and large churches and has the scars to show it. In a world of 'big, bigger, and biggest' Gene offers sane compassion and reminds readers that there are millions of people who will never attend a megachurch no matter how high its steeple may be. *In the Shadow of the Steeple* is a *must* reading for every pastor and board member. Buy two copies—one to keep and one to give away."

—Harold Ivan Smith
Author of numerous books; grief counselor
Kansas City

"In the Shadow of the Steeple is my kind of book. Having been a small-church pastor in my youthful ministry days (sometimes we had gusts of up to 17 in attendance), I am grateful for the insights received from Gene Williams and this outstanding and practical piece on church ministry. The vital role of smaller-church pastors cannot be ignored, since they represent 80 percent of the churches in the United States. I plan to recommend this book to all my seminar attendees."

—Stan Toler
Senior Pastor
Trinity Church of the Nazarene
Oklahoma City
For years taught seminars for John Maxwell's Injoy Group
Author of more than 50 books

"In the Shadow of the Steeple is an insightful look and consideration of the value of the smaller church. Gene Williams has given not only good analyses of the challenges facing churches of 125 and under but also thought-provoking admonition and talking points with positive results in view. As a district superintendent for 19 years, I can unreservedly commend this book to pastors and church boards as a point of renewal to once again realize that the future is as bright as the promises of God."

—Edmond P. Nash
District Superintendent
Kansas District, Church of the Nazarene
Wichita, Kansas

"*In the Shadow of the Steeple* is a book that needed to be written at a time when the pastor of the average or smaller church desperately needs encouragement. Gene Williams writes from his experience as pastor of small, average, and large congregations. His genuine compassion and support for all pastors is evident. Gene has dedicated his life to the call God gave him to 'feed my sheep.' As a pastor he did that for over 47 years. Since retiring from the active pulpit, he has dedicated his life to ministering to pastors and their spouses. This book was written to encourage pastors and to remind them that God has called them. He is not about to abandon them. I would recommend this book to all pastors and believe it will have a tremendous impact on the ministry of all who take the time to read it. Gene has lived the life of a pastor and has followed God's calling. He is now following a call to equip, encourage, and minister to pastors. The book should be a valuable addition for all who are in the ministry."

—Tex Reardon Jr.
Charlotte, North Carolina

"Many pastoral couples struggle in their family relationships because of time and activity pressures in their churches. Some feel like failures because of their church size, and they are constantly comparing themselves to other churches. Gene Williams lifts this feeling of inadequacy in this book, *In the Shadow of the Steeple,* thereby relieving some of the pressure on the parsonage family. This book will renew the heart and head of any struggling pastor."

—Gary Smalley
Author of *The DNA of Relationships*
Branson, Missouri

IN THE SHADOW OF THE STEEPLE

THE VITAL ROLE OF THE SMALLER CHURCH IN A MEGACHURCH WORLD

GENE WILLIAMS

Beacon Hill Press of Kansas City
Kansas City, Missouri

Copyright 2005
by Gene Williams and Beacon Hill Press of Kansas City

ISBN 083-412-1808

Printed in the
United States of America

Cover Design: Paul Franitza

All Scripture quotations not otherwise designated are from the *Holy Bible, New International Version*® (NIV®). Copyright © 1973, 1978, 1984 by International Bible Society. Used by permission of Zondervan Publishing House. All rights reserved.

Permission to quote from the following additional copyrighted version of the Bible is acknowledged with appreciation:

The *New King James Version* (NKJV). Copyright © 1979, 1980, 1982 Thomas Nelson, Inc.

Scripture quotations marked KJV are from the King James Version.

Library of Congress Cataloging-in-Publication Data

Williams, Gene, 1932-
    In the shadow of the steeple : the vital role of the smaller church in a megachurch world / Gene Williams.
        p. cm.
    ISBN 0-8341-2180-8 (pbk.)
    1. Small churches. I. Title.

    BV637 .8.W535 2005
    250—dc22

                                                    2005009759

10 9 8 7 6 5 4 3 2 1

CONTENTS

Foreword   9

Acknowledgments   11

Introduction   13

1. Potential   21

2. Purpose   31

3. Problems   39

4. Pleasure   55

5. Prospects   67

6. Pride   77

7. Power   89

8. Provision   99

9. Peace   109

Epilogue   117

1199

126864

13.804

FOREWORD

With the development of megachurch complexes with marvelous state-of-the-art facilities and well-polished programs along with the advent of highly gifted preachers on television, the expectations of people in the pew have risen dramatically. Pity, therefore, the poor pastor who feels that he or she cannot either compete with the undoubted abilities of the media preacher or imagine what it must be like to minister in a sanctuary as sumptuous as the one on the screen.

Add to this the fact that the problems experienced by many people today seem to outstrip those of previous generations, and accordingly pastors are expected to have expertise in a number of areas for which they feel desperately ill-equipped and which their forerunners in the pastorate would never have envisaged. The result can be feelings of despair, shattered self-image, and deep discouragement even to the point of abandoning the ministry, coupled with intense stress and the resultant tension at home.

Gene Williams knows all about the struggles of the modern pastor—particularly those who minister in smaller communities that can support only smaller churches. He's a seasoned practitioner who has ministered in a variety of situations and who has endeavored to encourage pastors for many years. It's out of an understanding heart and long experience that he writes *In the Shadow of the Steeple*. This is a book that is much needed, and I suspect it will be greatly appreciated by all those who, having spent their days encouraging others, need to sit down at the end of the day and derive a little encouragement for themselves. This book will do it.

—*Stuart Briscoe*

ACKNOWLEDGMENTS

Without the incredible encouragement and support from my wonderful wife, Joyce, this work never would have happened. Thank you, Honey, for the untold hours of your labor of love.

I also want to thank my friend Harold Ivan Smith, who sowed the seed that grew into this book. He saw a need and had faith that I would write something to encourage "pastors who labor in the shadow of large-church steeples." Here it is, Harold Ivan. Thanks for the challenge.

I thank my father, Virgil Williams, who taught me to love God unconditionally. He had no special talents but was a layman used of God because of his total commitment to our Father. He showed me the pure joy he found in serving our Lord.

Thanks, Daddy.

INTRODUCTION

Thousands of pastors across the country wrestle with the fact that they're pastoring small, struggling churches. They haven't caught on to the fact that there's a very special role in the Kingdom for such assignments. Many of them do double duty by working in secular jobs in addition to pastoring their churches—in order to support their families while they fulfill God's call on their lives.

In his classic book *The Purpose-Driven Church*, Pastor Rick Warren writes, "My greatest admiration is for the thousands of bivocational pastors who support themselves with a second job in order to shepherd churches that are too small to provide a full-time salary. They are the heroes of the faith, in my view. They will receive great honor in heaven" (19). I'm in total agreement with his statement.

If you're one of these pastors, please be reassured that you're admired and that God has a special place for you. The challenges you face in juggling schedules, commitments, and time constraints are enormous. Just remember: our Heavenly Father *will* reward your faithfulness.

With that in mind, please note that contrary to common opinion, bigger is not always better. Oh, I know that our society perpetuates the illusion that the larger anything is the better it is. The larger your house—the more successful you must be. Drive a big car or a sports-utility vehicle, and people think you're really doing well in the world. That analogy could go on and on. The problem is that it's not always true, and we'll see that as we examine this subject.

We've been so programmed in that frame of mind that we've infected the Church world with that same belief. As a result of this, many pastors have the mistaken idea that if his or

Success is making the most of the opportunity God has given to you to bring people into His kingdom.

her church doesn't have several hundred or thousand in attendance, he or she is not doing much for the Kingdom and must be a failure. Please hear me out. That simply is not true. Success in the Kingdom is not relegated to being the biggest church in your neighborhood. Your church may even be the smallest one. Success is making the most of the opportunity God has given to you to bring people into His kingdom.

I'm pleased that we have some megachurches. I thank God that some locations and situations are very fertile, have great pastors, and as a result produce great harvests. We're excited for these congregations. There are situations in which the large church makes a powerful statement to the non-Christian world. They speak to the popularity and power of our faith, and they carry great influence in their communities. I remember well the difference in the influence I had when I pastored a small church compared to what I experienced when I pastored a large congregation. It was a huge difference. In Gainesville, Florida, with my 12 members, I had little or no real influence on the community. In Wichita, Kansas, with over 2,000 members, it was a different story. So where it's possible, we need to strive for the greatness of the megachurch. The church needs to influence the community in which it lives.

Another problem for the small-church pastor is created by the glamour of television ministries. Those churches with huge budgets, breathtaking facilities, and professional or near-professional talent have raised unreasonable expectations in the minds of many people. The result is increased pressure on pastors to produce a "mini" television-type service using their small-church talents and limited resources. What are the consequences? Pastors who are frustrated—and as a result they struggle with their call to minister and with their local assignment.

I'm pleased that we're able to occupy at least some of the television airtime with the message of Jesus. I have been deeply involved in media ministry and realize the impact it can have for the Kingdom on a community.

However, never—and I mean *never*—underestimate the importance of the smaller church that ministers in the shadow of the steeple of the big church. A pastor who takes his or her church from 50 to 60 may have accomplished as much or more for God as the one who takes his or her church from 2,500 to 3,000. Remember the parable of the sower (Matt. 13:3-9). The environment and soil kept some of it from producing 100-fold. Was the 30-fold ground successful? It was 30 times better than nothing! Sometimes to produce *anything* in one's location and circumstances is worthy of praise.

I'm not saying that we should ever be satisfied with zero growth. May God help us never to be content with no harvest. There's no room for complacency in the work of the Kingdom. However, I'm saying that there are situations and circumstances when conditions may not be conducive to producing a large crowd. Regardless, we can always find joy in what we accomplish for Jesus. The key is to honestly do our best for the One who believed in us and gave us the opportunity to serve Him.

As I write these lines, the Kansas wheat harvest is in full swing. Some of the farmers' storage bins are bursting at the seams. Others are wondering if they'll be able to survive. The weather has played havoc with them. While all of them want a great harvest, some farmers are glad to put anything into their bins. Under difficult conditions, harvesting anything may be a major accomplishment, and it will also enable the farmer to continue farming.

Let's change the analogy. I'm a real baseball fan. I played ball until my body said, "No more!" So you know that I've attended and participated in a lot of games. Over these years I've observed some great power hitters. When a baseball player is hitting home runs, he usually makes the headlines. That's especially true if he hits a grand slam to win the game. In all the years I've followed baseball, there have been very few "singles hitters" in the headlines. Why not? Singles are not as glamorous as home runs. Are they important? You know the answer to that. More games are won by singles hitters than by home-run hitters. Singles are just not as emotionally exciting. The critical issue is this: *Get a hit of some kind.*

If we bring that analogy into the church world, we see that the single-hitters—pastors of smaller churches—win more people to Jesus than the power pastors. Isn't it wonderful that we're on the same team with the same Manager, working for the same purpose?

I've lived on both sides of this issue. Pastoring a church in a basement room in Hohenwald, Tennessee, was some kind of an experience. I'll never forget that first Sunday when 23 people showed up for worship and sat on those homemade benches. We had church, and God came to meet our hearts. You won't be surprised when I tell you that within six months we had over 100 in attendance.

The church I pastored in Mirable, Missouri, was 10 miles from the closest paved road, in the heart of farm country. However, wonderful people lived on those farms, and they drove the dirt roads to be in God's presence. It was richly rewarding to spend all day every Sunday with those great people.

Then, after moving halfway across the country to Sebring, Florida, I'll never forget hearing the words "Nobody will come. We can't get them to come to our little church." And they were right. Nobody would come—until something happened. When the 41 people who met us that first Sunday came fully alive, the people did come. In fact, we couldn't get all of them into the building. When we give people a reason to come to church, they'll come.

You probably never heard of Princeton, Florida. Until recently, it didn't even have a traffic light. There was one small restaurant and a hardware store. That was it. Almost everyone in that area was involved in farming and lived in the surrounding area. There were a lot of people, however, north of Princeton in Miami and south of Princeton in Homestead. So we decided to create an atmosphere of excitement. Then we watched them drive in from all over south Florida— 500 on an average Sunday.

We can find pleasure and joy wherever God puts us.

I've reviewed the list of some of the places I pastored to let you know that I've been there. I had the pleasure of pastoring what might be called minichurches and the joy of pastoring a major church in Wichita, Kansas, for over 26 years. Please hear me when I say that *we can find pleasure and joy wherever God puts us.*

I look back on some of those smaller assignments, and wonderful memories come to mind. Yes, there were problems, and we'll look at some of those. But I had some great experiences in those small churches that God had entrusted to me. By His grace, any of us can make a difference in any community He assigns to us by spreading the joy of His will for our lives.

On the cover of his book *Small, Strong Congregations* Kennon Callahan states,

> The twenty-first century is the century of small, strong congregations. More people will be drawn to small, strong congregations than any other kind of congregation. Yes, there are mega-congregations; their number is increasing greatly. Nevertheless, across the planet, the vast majority of

I finally admitted that I had a problem— a problem that would not be solved with a change in geography. What was needed was a change in me.

—Steve Bierly

congregations will be small and strong, and the vast majority of people will be in these congregations.

In his book *How to Thrive as a Small-Church Pastor,* Steve Bierly described how he learned to make the most of his assignment as the pastor of a small church. After relating several things that began happening that he could not explain away, he concluded,

> I no longer felt I had a significant part to play in God's plans for His kingdom. The small church had my ambitions and dreams effectively contained in the confines of its four walls. My life seemed as though it was going to be bound up with the problems, concerns and complaints of small groups of people forever. There was no escape. Even if I moved, chances were that I would wind up in a small church. I finally admitted that I had a problem—a problem that would not be solved with a change in geography. What was needed was a change in me (12).

I really admire that transparent statement acknowledging, *What was needed was a change in me.* There are multiplied thousands of pastors who labor for the Lord in small churches. Many of these are in the shadow of a huge steeple, and that just adds to their struggles. Sometimes the challenges seem to be overwhelming.

What's the answer? A change in *me!* God gave the assignment to pastor a smaller church to someone He believes can fulfill that calling. So give the Kingdom everything you have, but don't let the fact that you're not running in the hundreds or thousands rob you of the joy of serving God with everything you have right where you are. God has complimented you by entrusting into your care some of those for whom He died. He believes in you. Now you must believe in yourself.

In the closing chapter of *The Purpose-Driven Church*, Pastor Warren admonishes pastors, "Don't worry about the growth of your church. Focus on fulfilling the purpose of your church" (394). There's a reason for every church to exist and a purpose for it to carry out. Rather than surrendering to the discouragement that often accompanies pastoring small churches, focus on what God has given you the privilege of doing: representing Him.

We're a success-focused society. And the inference is that we're not successful unless we multiply our numbers. Again, I turn to Pastor Warren: "Successful ministry is building the church on the purposes of God in the power of the Holy Spirit and expecting the results from God" (397). *Success is building the church on the purposes of God.* And what is that purpose? To introduce people to Jesus. As you will read later in this book, many people will never enter the megachurch. They're intimidated by the size of the crowds of people who attend there. In the shadow of the high steeple of the huge churches are people who will never know Jesus unless someone is faithful to maximize the opportunity to pastor the small churches.

Faithfulness to the call of God is the key to making the most of the privilege of being the pastor serving the small congregation. And God has given that privilege to you along with His promise to enable you to make the most of it.

Again, I want to make it clear that the joy of faithfulness to the call does not depend on the numerical outcome. Joy comes from consistently persevering to do the very best job possible to minister in the assignment to which God calls you. I can honestly say that I felt and experienced just as much joy while being faithful to minister in the very small churches as I did when I pastored a very large church in which I was on television each week.

I understand the struggles many small-church pastors encounter. However, I can testify that there is joy to be realized in any field of service to which God calls us. Our pleasure comes from hearing Him say, "Well done, good and faithful servant!" (Matt. 25:21).

1
POTENTIAL
There's enormous potential
in the shadow of the steeple.

Pastor Dale left for church early that Sunday morning. He always wanted to arrive in plenty of time to make sure the air conditioner was working well and everything was ready for whoever might show up. He was really struggling with his call to preach. He kept thinking, *If I'm truly called, why is my church not growing like the megachurch down the street?* As he drove past the huge worship center, he got caught in the traffic as police directed traffic into the giant parking lot in order to keep the flow moving. It seemed to him that everybody in town was headed to the big church.

Finally he got out of the traffic and moved into his church's empty little parking lot, wondering if anybody would be there. What a difference! *Why is everybody going to the big church? What's wrong with us—me?*

Pastor Dale was truly struggling internally. He really loved God and wanted to serve Him. But it just seemed as though he was not making a difference. His small congregation seemed to struggle just to exist when compared to the big church down the street. He really was distressed because it seemed as though everyone wanted to attend the big church.

The fact is, they're not all *going to the megachurch.* In reality, on any given Sunday less than 25 percent of the people in North America attend *any* church. In his book *Giant Awakenings* Thom Rainer quotes two important studies on church life in

America. Such studies show that 44 percent of the population is solidly unchurched. Another study shows that 71 percent of the United States population is unaffiliated with a church or are Christians in name only. This simply means that although it may appear that everybody is going to the giant church, most people in every community are still at home sleeping in or reading the Sunday paper. Rainer further notes that C. Peter Wagner estimates the unchurched population in America may be as high as 55 percent. People may claim that the United States is still a Christian nation, but if church attendance is part of that picture, we have a serious problem. Thank God for the faithful millions who attend regularly—but there are multiple millions more who desperately need a church home.

In the shadow of the steeple of any church on any given Sunday there will be enough people staying home to fill every house of worship to overflowing if they could just be motivated to attend. We have preconceived ideas of what's happening in the church world. Maybe it's time we went to the bottom line and simply realized that the fields are still "white unto harvest" and that we have a lot of work to do.

In the Introduction to this book I referred to the Kansas wheat harvest. Some of those farmers work with thousands of acres of wheat with several combines to bring in the harvest. Suppose an ambitious farmer wants to find some land on which he or she can grow a wheat crop. Should this farmer pursue his or her dream? The farmer doesn't have thousands of acres and unlimited resources but does have land and desire. The facts are that most of the huge spreads began as small farms. Hard work and perseverance have paid off for every successful farmer. Still, many farmers never become part of the corporate world. They remain "family farms" and enjoy making the most of what they have.

That same situation is true in the church world. While some church plants grow into megachurches, there will always be a place for the "family church." Many people are drawn to a church where they can be individuals and not just part of a crowd.

In their research work *Beyond the Ordinary: Ten Strengths of U.S. Congregations,* Cynthia Woolever and Deborah Bruce state that their research points out that "Worshipers in small congregations have a greater sense of belonging than participants in large congregations" (50).

Over the years of pastoring a large church, I was told many times, "Pastor, your church is too large for us. We just can't get involved in a big church." Some people are simply inhibited by large crowds. They're much more comfortable in the intimate setting of a small congregation.

Cheers was a hit television comedy that took place in a neighborhood bar. The theme song for that program had a line in it that pointed out that people want to go "where everybody knows your name." Although the bar setting of that program is certainly undesirable, I do know that *people enjoy going where they're called by their names.* Regardless of how gifted a pastor may be, if he or she has thousands to minister to, there's no way to call them all by name. My last church was a far cry from a megachurch, but frankly the words "brother" and "sister" came in handy on many occasions when I recognized faces but drew blanks on names.

When I was pastoring a small church, I knew the names of all of my people and loved looking them in the eye when using their favorite nickname. That intimacy, which is just not possible in the large church, is attractive to many. They respond positively to the family setting rather than the convention atmosphere. A warm, small worship center that shows sincere interest is always attractive. You may not have many people at present, but you will—because *wherever there are*

Wherever there are people, we can build a church.

people, we can build a church. All we need is a desire to bring people to Jesus, the will to work hard, and people.

A building of some kind would be nice, but even that is not absolutely necessary to have a good church. On a mission trip to Swaziland, South Africa, a few years ago I had the privilege of worshiping with a congregation who met under a giant tree. They had no building—they simply met each Sunday morning in the shade of that tree. Such a place is not without problems. This was quickly revealed when a nonbelieving farmer drove his cattle nearby. But even that incident did not drive away God's presence. There were people there, and God had motivated a native pastor to care for them as he provided their spiritual nourishment. It was not easy, but carrying the Cross was not comfortable for Jesus either. That African pastor had caught that same Spirit. He willingly paid the price for His people to experience the peace for which Jesus had died.

> *There are no small assignments in God's kingdom.*

I understand that it's not easy to be motivated by a small crowd. Fortunately for me, an early ministry mentor told me, "Preach like you have 1,000, and take up an offering like you have 10,000." I understood what he was saying. What we're doing is important. *There are no small assignments in God's kingdom.* Although sometimes it may seem that we need to furnish all the energy in a service, He who called us will equip us to carry out our assignment. The laypeople may seem to be discouraged. But by God's grace and in His strength we can bring into His presence those with whom God has entrusted us.

We may not have talented musicians to help in every assignment. In fact, in some situations there may not be much music at all. In that case we have a choice. We can give up on the situation or become innovative. I urge you to try to be creative. In one of my early churches we gathered to worship in a basement whose dampness had wreaked havoc on the piano. It was so out of tune that it sounded awful. But that was OK—we rarely had anyone to play it anyway.

I was looking for help with the piano when a member told me that he knew someone who could play a guitar. Just as a "Good!" came out of my mouth, she qualified her statement by telling me the person was blind. Then she asked, "Will that be a problem?" Of course I said, "No." I simply decided to lead him down the steps into our "sanctuary" and sing whatever songs he could play. We had some interesting experiences.

To this day, every time I hear the song "Come and Dine," I get a mental picture of that congregation. You see, that was my blind guitarist's favorite song. The congregation had missed out on the musical talents that hang around nearby Nashville. But it did not bother them at all. We made the most of our opportunities and experienced results. There were people in our neighborhood, and we brought them into the building and carried them into the presence of Jesus.

The very fact that Satan works so hard to discourage the "Pastor Dales" of this world should be an encouragement. Please note—*Satan never wastes time discouraging people who are not in a position to make a difference.* Thousands of Christian workers, pastors, missionaries, singers, teachers, and so on have their roots in a small church somewhere. We'll address this point later. Just be assured that pastors of small churches are in a position to make a significant difference. Face your discouragement with that awareness, and determine to move on so you can enjoy God's blessings.

You may feel opposed, as I did when I planted a new church in Gainesville, Florida. It was not an easy assignment. It got tougher when some non-Christians who lived nearby got up a petition to keep the church from moving into their neighborhood. At that time I was young, naive, and just didn't know I was supposed to quit when opposition came. Sometimes I believe a tough hide is a major part of pastoral survival.

God had laid that neighborhood on my heart. There were people there for whom Jesus had died. Most of them were not going to the big downtown churches. So I had the opportunity to bring to their doorsteps the good news of Jesus' love for them. Pastoring that baby church became a wonderful experience as the people responded to us.

Warm Christian love always melts cold hearts.

What about the petition? Somewhere along the way it got lost. I began to get acquainted with the people. Soon the very family who had started the opposition were coming across the street to worship with us. Warm Christian love always melts cold hearts. I wonder how many difficult situations could become positive experiences if they were faced firmly with the strength of the Lord.

There's a special place in the Kingdom for smaller churches. While the exact numbers may never be known, John Vaughan (with Church Growth Today, headquartered in Bolivar, Missouri) reports that of the over 400,000 churches in the United States, 80 percent of them average fewer than 200 in attendance. It has been estimated that 50 percent run fewer than 50. On the other end of the spectrum, less than 1 percent of the churches in the United States have over 2,000 in attendance. According to Dr. Vaughan, this number is increasing at the rate of one new 2,000-member church every three days. Praise God for this progress! This is a vast improvement over 1970, when, as Dr. Vaughan reports, there were only 10 non-Catholic churches in the United States that ran 2,000 or more in attendance. There are now 870 churches in this category.

Still, the overwhelming number of churches remains on the

smaller end of the scale. Why are there so many churches on the lower end of the attendance scale? There's a myriad of reasons, and I won't begin to attempt to explain all of them or to prescribe cures for them. However, we must acknowledge a few of them.

- In some situations, changes in the population have a detrimental effect. The megachurch has a visibility that invites people to drive there. Hence, it continues to thrive.
- The smaller churches in the shadow of those larger ones are left to minister to the faithful who have been attending for years and a few who still live in the neighborhood.
- In some cases there's no vision for change. The buildings and programs still reflect "the good old days." It's extremely difficult to reach today's generation with ancient methods. Some churches even smell old and musty, and there's certainly nothing attractive about that.
- Limitations in leadership restrict the number of people who can be reached. This can be a pastoral weakness or in many instances a deficiency in lay leadership.
- Some people just like to worship in a smaller, more intimate setting and don't feel the urgency to grow. New people may be a threat to their comfort zones. However, such shortsighted people are still worthy of God's love and need to be cared for and challenged.

That's just a small overview of some reasons a smaller church can find a place even in the shadow of a large steeple. Some things are signs of church health just as weight, pulse, and blood pressure measure physical health. The following are what I believe are some signs of a healthy church:

- Absolute commitment to and communication of God's Word.
- Genuine love between the pastor and the people, and love between the people.

• A commitment to expend whatever energy, resources, and effort it takes to reach the people for whom Jesus died.

You can't keep a healthy church from growing.

Where these health signs are good, the church will be healthy. *And you can't keep a healthy church from growing.* It may never become a megachurch, but it has a vital role in the kingdom of God. Remember: not all ballplayers are home-run hitters. But the game would not be won without the players who hit singles. If you're a "singles hitter," there are people counting on you, and you can take pride in what God enables you to be.

The morning Pastor Dale drove by the megachurch, he was actually getting on base to help win the game for the same team Manager for whom the large-church pastor was playing. So take heart, all of you "Pastor Dales." Even though you may not feel you're hitting any over the fence, God has a game plan that's out of this world!

Let me give you an example of what God wants to do. The area around Kansas City has thousands of churches that proclaim God's love. Some of those raise a very high steeple. Several qualify as megachurches by their thousands in attendance. So why start another small church? Because there are multitudes of people who are not attending anywhere, and God loves them too.

When Dorzell King Jr. first approached Keith Wright, all he wanted was an opportunity to preach. He had recently graduated from Mid-America Nazarene University in Olathe, Kansas, just a few miles from Kansas City, and wanted to do what God had called him to do. They discussed planting a church in a blue-collar racially mixed neighborhood. Dr. Wright had access to an old abandoned building in that area that could be used for their meetings.

The building was cleaned up, and word began to spread about the new church. Would anyone come? After all, there are great churches all around. Would they come! Oh, yes! In fact, by the end of the first year they had to find a larger building to hold the 250-plus people who showed up regularly each Sunday morning.

My son, Steve, was the first one to tell me about Risen Lamb International Church of the Nazarene. He and his wife, Kelly, who had been attending a megachurch in the area, just happened to attend one Sunday. They fell in love with Risen Lamb Church. Although it was only a fraction of the size of the church they had been attending, there was something special about that place. Steve, who has been raised in church, says, "It is so much fun to go to church." He loves the spirit of that young pastor, who has caught the joy of serving God wherever he can.

God's plan is to reach the people in your neighborhood who will never attend the huge church. And He has chosen you to be His instrument to draw them to His heart. God tailor-makes an opportunity for everyone to come into the Kingdom. Your church is critical to the success of that plan. *Whether your neighborhood is blue collar, white collar, or no collar, since people are there, the potential is available for you to have an awesome church.*

POINTS TO PONDER

1. The majority of people in your neighborhood are not attending the megachurch. What does this mean to you in your assignment?
2. Most people prefer to be part of a personalized experience. How does this help in the ministry of a small church?
3. What is the health quotient of your church?
4. What does it mean to you personally that Jesus has chosen you to be His instrument to reach people for whom He died?

Scripture

I will build my church, and the gates of Hades will not over-come it (Matt. 16:18).

Prayer

Dear Father, You planted this church as a seed of Your love. You promised to bless it in spite of all of the difficulties it might face. I want to lead our church to be what You want it to be. I give myself to You. Help my church to grow into the fullness of Your plan so that we may glorify Your name. In Jesus' name. Amen.

2
PURPOSE

**There's a purpose to be discovered
in the shadow of the steeple.**

As the crowd of pastors gathered for a special meeting, Pastor Ray felt more and more alone. They had come together to rally the strength of the churches behind a community issue. It was obvious where the real strength was—the four largest congregations in the city. Still, he, like all the pastors in town, had been invited, and he wanted to be a part of this effort.

Everyone paid special attention when the large-church pastors came near. Pastor Ray wondered if anyone even knew he was there. Oh, they spoke kind "hellos," and three other pastors finally sat at his table. Their conversation was relaxed and courteous. But he didn't know their names, and it soon became obvious that they really didn't know each other. They were just there. They, too, had received the invitation.

As the meeting rolled on, Pastor Ray caught himself wondering, *Why am I here? Would anyone even miss me if we closed up my little church and sent everyone to the megachurch six blocks away?* He was really struggling with why his small church even existed. This issue had been gnawing away at him as he watched the shadow of the steeple of the larger church get ever longer and bigger. He worked hard to get his attendance over 60. It seemed that people just naturally flowed to the big church, which was running over 2,000 in attendance. Why not just let his 62 go to the large church and make it 2,062? To his amazement the other pastors at his table began to express some of the same feelings. "Why not just let the big get bigger and get out of their way?"

Well, Pastor Ray, let me tell you why. *There's a vital place in the Kingdom for every church.* And to adapt a saying concerning poor people, God must have a special place in His heart for small churches, because there are so many.

Sometimes it helps if we get a clear picture of the situation. I really think it helps pastors of small churches to realize that the overwhelming majority of churches are anything but giants. But tragically, the majority of North American churches are not growing.

It's exciting to know about some megachurches that are virtually bursting at the seams. Churches of 15,000-20,000, while few in number, prove that enormous growth can happen. It's wonderful to see what's happening at places like Lakewood Church in Houston. John Vaughan states that in 2004 Lakewood was the largest and fastest-growing church in the United States. The congregation began meeting in a feed store and is now running a total of 30,000 in its four services. The kingdom of God has some 100-fold fields. We're pleased when that happens, and this should excite us. However, we don't dare to let our failure to reach that high pinnacle become a weapon of defeat. Suppose all mountain climbers had to reach the peak of Mount Everest or else consider themselves to be failures. Obviously, there would be many more failures than successes. So it is in ministry. There are many more churches on the lower-level mountains of attendance, but the important thing is to keep climbing.

We must learn to make the most of whatever opportunity we have. On a visit to Singapore, my wife, Joyce, and I had the privilege of worshiping at City Harvest Church. Their sanctuary is 70 feet underground and seats 2,500. Because space is at a premium, they have very little parking provided. However, by having multiple services in numerous languages, this church that started in 1988 with 20 people now reaches over 15,000 per week. The best news is that 300-400 each week are being brought into the Kingdom there. This is happening in a country that's 60 percent Buddhist.

A pessimist might say, "So, they're growing and winning everyone. Why should we waste our efforts? Why not get out of their way and let them have everyone?" Let me tell you why not: not everyone is attending City Harvest. *There's no way a few large churches can care for all of those for whom Jesus died.* There are a number of small Christian churches in Singapore that could be tempted to fold—to leave ministry to City Harvest. However, this city, which is bound to an island, has no fewer than 5.5 million people. Jesus died for all of them. Most will not go to City Harvest Church. The best chance of reaching them is through multiple healthy smaller churches that lift up Jesus.

What's the purpose of the smaller church? It's very simple— to lift up Jesus and enable those not drawn to the atmosphere of the huge church to come to a personal relationship with Him.

Maybe we need to clearly understand what any church's purpose is. Let there be no mistake. The purpose is the same— regardless of its size. We may better understand the purpose if we take a quick look at what it's not.

- It's not to build beautiful buildings. Nonbelievers can do that for their own purposes.
- It's not just to have great programs. Many organizations and entertainers can do that.
- It's not even to have great worship experiences. Sometimes they can become self-centered.
- It's not simply to provide religious activities. Many other religions do that.

Yes—

- Beautiful buildings are an asset and nice to have wherever it's possible.
- Great programs are wonderful experiences and tools to use in reaching new people.

- Great worship experiences can be special times when we're lifted into the presence of God.
- Religious activities certainly have a place in our lives.

But there must be no question that the purpose of the church, regardless of its size, is to lift up Jesus, who said, "When I am lifted up from the earth, [I] will draw all men to myself" (John 12:32).

The megachurch may do this, but so can any church of any size. The lifting-up of Jesus is not relegated to a certain-size church. *Our satisfaction should come not just from the "number of heads in the house" but from the number of hearts at the foot of the Cross.*

The size of the church may seem to make it easier to reach people, but research shows that small churches have a powerful impact on individual lives. In their book *Beyond the Ordinary: 10 Strengths of U.S. Congregations,* Cynthia Woolever and Deborah Bruce make a strong case for the effectiveness of the smaller church. The U.S. Congregational Life Survey, from which they draw their conclusions, involved 300,000 worshipers in over 2,000 congregations. Every "Pastor Ray" needs to take a good look at this research. It may very well explain why God has planted so many churches that average fewer than 100 in attendance. Let me be quick to add that I don't believe He planted them to abandon them to struggle on their own. God intends for every church to be effective, since He sent His only Son to die for them. *We must be discontented if people are not being saved.* Again, our purpose, regardless of size or location, is to bring people to Jesus. No one should find comfort in the 80 percent of churches that are stagnant or declining. Barrenness is the curse of the church, not size.

Barrenness is the curse of the church, not size.

For many years I was a member of a ministerial board to which young pastors report as they await ordination. One young man who was pastoring in a very difficult situation came before that board for four straight years without having led one single person to Jesus. Frankly, I could not let that slide any longer, so I confronted him as kindly as possible. My purpose was to awaken him, not destroy him. So I simply asked, "What did you do with the last 52 weeks during which God entrusted that community to your care? I believe I could have found a boy or girl and won him or her to Jesus." I left it at that.

The following year he came to me and asked for forgiveness. I didn't understand what that was all about, but he went on to explain. He said, "Last year you put me on the spot when you asked me to account for the way I had spent the past year. I was very angry and upset with you. However, on the way home from that meeting, God opened my eyes. Just for the record, I had the privilege of leading five new people into the Kingdom." He was pleased, I was pleased, but most of all I was sure God was pleased. A tiny church had experienced what churches are designed to do—win people to Jesus.

In biblical days barrenness was heartbreaking and sometimes considered to be a curse. In Gen. 15 we read that Abraham was desperate to have a child. In 1 Sam. 1 Hannah was in deep distress because of her barrenness and agonized in prayer until God gave a son to her. There were many others who were in despair until they had children. Our hearts should break in the same way today. May we never be comfortable with barrenness. Our purpose is to have children born into the Kingdom. And the potential for this is all around us. While some situations are more difficult than others, we must never become satisfied with barrenness.

One question that must be considered in order to understand the small church's purpose is "Do small, midsize, and large congregations differ in their spiritual strength?" According to the study upon which *Beyond the Ordinary* is based, they do. On four of five elements used to comprise a "growing spiritual index," small congregations achieved higher scores than larger congregations (20).

Two other statements from that study help us to understand why God has so many small churches. "Worshipers in midsize and larger congregations are more dissatisfied with the spiritual nurture that they receive than those in smaller congregations. Secondly, smaller congregations are more likely than larger congregations to hold services that help worshipers with their everyday lives" (32). The small church fills a critical place in the lives of those who choose to worship in that smaller setting.

Some people get lost in the crowd at the megachurch, becoming spiritually anonymous. I received a phone call from a local mortician wanting me to conduct a funeral. The service was for a lady I had never met. Because of that, I asked why I had been asked to speak. The mortician explained that this lady worked for one of the wealthiest people in our city, and he wanted me to conduct her service.

I called that prominent businessman and asked, "Why did you ask me to speak?" I'll never forget his response. "Gene," he said, "You were her pastor. You just never met her, because she would slip into your services late and leave before the benediction. She was our maid and cook. She wanted to always have Sunday dinner ready by 1 P.M. She loved your preaching but didn't want to get involved." So she worshiped anonymously. And that's easy to do in a congregation of 1,400 people.

Not everyone gets lost in the crowd of a large church. Please note that many people soar on the sheer power of the numbers. But there are many who find it easy to go through the motions. They never come face-to-face with the busy pastor and the truth that he or she preaches. So they are able to hide behind a spiritual facade in their anonymity.

Obviously, in a small church it's hard to hide. When I pastored smaller churches, I watched people who thought they were anonymous as they worked on their palm pilots or whatever. I could tell when they were sleepy or alert, because I have a habit of looking my congregation in the eyes. However, later when I preached to over 1,400, some sat so far back I could hardly see their faces. So they were able to worship anonymously as the lady I mentioned earlier. To this day I find it easier to influence people in a smaller, more intimate setting than in a huge crowd.

The smaller church must be fully alive, but it should never assume that it's not important. Multitudes of Christian leaders had their roots in small churches. The intimate contact they had with their pastors fanned the flame of God's fire that had been ignited in their hearts. Spending top-quality time with a pastor who rejoices in God's plan threw fuel on the fire as those future leaders anticipated being used of God. Whatever the call of God might be, the intimate contact that can happen only in a small church was critical to the formation and maturing of those who would carry on the work of the Kingdom.

In the giant shadow of the large-church steeple there's a vital role to be played for those who lead small congregations into the presence of the Lord. It isn't that pastors of large churches can't have that influence—I'm sure many do. However, when we have the responsibility for thousands of people and the corresponding responsibilities for a huge complex, there's very little time for intimate personal experiences. The times when megachurch pastors can enjoy relationships that are normal, everyday occurrences to small-church pastors are few and far between.

So, Pastor Ray, why are you still leading that church of 62? Because God has confidence in you and wants you to pass on His love to people who might otherwise get lost in a crowd. And we find great joy in bringing those hearts to the foot of the Cross. Just never be satisfied to be barren of new babes in Christ.

POINTS TO PONDER

1. How large must a church be to be used of God to change lives? What does this say to you?

2. Think this through: Our satisfaction should come, not from the number of heads in the house, but from the number of hearts at the foot of the Cross. How does this statement speak to your heart?

3. Consider: The curse of any church is barrenness. We must never become comfortable with this affliction. How many spiritual children have you birthed in the last year?

4. Consider: It's easy to get lost in the crowd and go through some religious ritual. What does this mean to the smaller church?

Scripture

Go and make disciples of all nations, baptizing them in them in the name of the Father and of the Son and of the Holy Spirit, and teaching them to obey everything I have commanded you. And surely I am with you always, to the very end of the age (Matt. 28:19-20).

Prayer

Dear Father, I want to fulfill the purpose You have for me and the church You have given to me to pastor. I want to be a change agent for the people in this community of opportunity. Help me to bring into the family of believers those for whom You died. Please, God—deliver me from the curse of barrenness. In Your Son's name I pray. Amen.

3
PROBLEMS

**There will be problems in the
shadow of the steeple.**

"I don't like the way things are going. I resign." And with that
angry statement, our treasurer got up and walked out. I had
been pastor at that little church for six months. We were reaching out to new people and growing. In fact, we had already
doubled in size from the 23 I met the first Sunday I came to
pastor. So this explosion in our Sunday afternoon board meeting caught me by complete surprise.

I was young—19. That was my first church, and I was naive,
green as a gourd, immature, inexperienced—all the adjectives
you could imagine. But I knew I was there by divine appointment. So in keeping with His divine promises, God helped me
to stay calm. I really think I shocked that dear lady when I
calmly replied, "I'm sorry you feel that way. I'll be by later to
pick up the books." I did not try to talk her out of her decision.
In fact, I think that's what shocked her.

I should have been intimidated. She was the only person in
that tiny church in Hohenwald, Tennessee, with a full-time job.
I'm sure that most of my meager salary came from her tithe.
But for some divine reason, I had an awesome calm. I confess,
I did not think the situation through. If I had, I may have tried
to placate that dear lady. Fortunately for the church, I reacted
under the clear guidance of the Holy Spirit. I was calm, kind,
and courteous but firm in my response.

You won't be surprised when I tell you that following that

exchange almost every member of the board came to me and thanked me for the way I had handled the situation. One member went on to say, "She's run off every pastor we've ever had." Since that lady was the biggest contributor by far, she had assumed the role of "church boss." I do have to add, however, that after an absence of several weeks and watching the church continue to thrive, she returned to be a part of the congregation. As He always does, God had funneled our financial needs through someone else. So she saw the church moving on without her and didn't want to get totally left behind.

Let me assure you that there can be serious problems in the larger church as well. While pastoring a very large church, I was approached one Sunday morning by a very disgruntled member. It was just before the service began, and I was sitting on the platform. The choir was entering, and the music was playing. He came to the edge of the platform and motioned for me to come to him. I had no idea what was going to happen.

There will be problems anywhere we find people.

This disturbed man took me by the lapels of my coat, pulled me close, and said, "I ought to kill you." He was so angry that there was fire in his eyes.

Since I was not sure exactly what to do, I quietly said, "I'm sorry you feel that way. But it's time for the service to begin. Could we talk later?" I had a problem in the big church. Fortunately, it was resolved without disruption. But try to preach after experiencing such an encounter just minutes before entering the pulpit!

There will be problems anywhere we find people. The small church has no corner on this. However, let's look at some of the most prominent problems small churches encounter.

PROBLEMS WITH PEOPLE

One of the major problems of pastors of small churches is the strong-willed member who wants to run the church. Guess what! Larger churches have them too! No one size has a monopoly on dominant personalities. The difference is that in the small church the pastor usually has to face the situation without much support from the congregation. The "church boss" has a way of intimidating everyone. In most cases, the "ruler's" family becomes a controlling cell who sees to it that the ruler's wishes are carried out. Other people have some fear of that clan, so the pastor faces them alone. In the megachurch there's usually a strong support group for the pastor. However, even then it still hurts the Body of Christ when a strong-willed saint insists on things being done his or her way.

I'm convinced that personality issues are the major problems small churches face. As the "church boss" directs or dismantles a congregation, he or she influences everything that happens at that church. What many "church bosses" have never realized is that the one who influences the decisions takes responsibility for the outcome.

Throughout such times of conflict the atmosphere in the congregation usually becomes tense and cold. It's hard to relax and open our hearts and minds to the presence of the Holy Spirit when we're concerned about offending "the boss." The entire congregation, including the pastor, may be found looking over their shoulders to see how the power broker is responding. In those churches where one or two people are in charge, you can describe the atmosphere by editing an old family line: "If Mama ain't happy, ain't nobody happy." In many churches "If the church boss ain't happy, ain't nobody happy." And, I might add, it's very difficult to experience the presence of God.

As a result of such tension, the church will stay small and struggle to survive. It's sad but true to say that I have encoun-

If the church is a battleground rather than a sanctuary, very few new people will ever show up.

tered situations in which the power brokers let it be known that they did not want a lot of new people coming in and taking over "their church." They don't need to worry. *If the church is a battleground rather than a sanctuary, very few new people will ever show up.*

The small-church pastor should not be tempted to think, *If only I pastored a larger church, I wouldn't have these problems.* Let me assure you that numbers only multiply the opportunity for misunderstandings to arise. Instead of one strong personality with which you must deal, some large-church pastors must work with a number of potential hotheads. You can be sure that the bigger the church is, the larger the problems will be. Wherever there are people, you can build a church. But you can also be sure that won't happen without problems.

I acted as an arbitrator in a situation at a megachurch in which a very charismatic Sunday School teacher led his entire class in rebellion against the kind, loving senior pastor. The pastor had reached out to some attendees with which the teacher had issues. The teacher did not feel that those people should be encouraged to keep coming to the church. In fact, he wanted the pastor to tell them they could not return. That teacher was able to rally the class leadership to his cause and created a power structure to oppose the pastor who dared to believe that there's room in the Kingdom for everyone.

After months of wrestling over the situation, the church board clearly sided with the senior pastor and called for me to sit in with an arbitration committee. That Sunday School teacher was so "dug in" to his position that there was no changing him. He was absolutely inflexible. The end result was that over 200 people left the church.

"So what?" you might say. Several other hundreds remained. Yes, that's very true. But a brokenhearted pastor was left to lead that congregation. Although this situation occurred quite a few years ago, that "shepherd" is still hurting over the sheep who left his fold. The church has long since recovered the number of people who were lost—but some hurts seem to never completely heal.

You can be sure: whether your church steeple is a tall one or you're in the shadow of one, it doesn't matter. *Wherever there are people, there will always be personality clashes.*

PROBLEMS WITH FINANCES

Another problem that perplexes many small churches is the area of finances. You can naturally expect that a small number of people will have less money to invest in the Kingdom. And their resources may not always meet the demand. Most pastors of small churches are poorly paid financially, and many are bivocational. There's usually very little equipment and few resources with which to work. That can create some real problems in our high-tech world. Occasionally one or two people are able to prevent financial problems. But please note—in some situations this is a formula for trouble. According to an old saying, "He who signs the checks calls the shots." Blessed is the man or woman who is able to give generously and does so to the glory of God.

It's not unusual for persons of wealth to fail to recognize that God wants to use them to finance His work in the local church. Many of them reason, "If I tithe all my income on the local level, it will put the church's finances out of balance." Yes, I've actually heard those words. Also, it's not unusual for a person of means to give with "strings attached" to a special project.

By doing so they miss the concept that their tithe is of no greater ultimate value than that of the common laborer who brings his or her 10 percent to the storehouse.

One thing you can be sure of is that *God will always find someone to finance His work.* He expects the church to operate within its means. In a small congregation, obligations must be kept under control. It's essential to prepare and follow a budget. However, a pastor might be tempted to think, *If only we had the money of the big church down the street, we wouldn't have to worry about money.* Think again! The financial pressure at the megachurch can be enormous. I know of a church with a very large steeple that has had to cut staff personnel and eliminate some programs because of economic problems in that community. I remember very well that during one economic downturn the very large church I was pastoring at the time was seriously behind in bills.

While some churches raise millions and the smaller churches may only raise thousands, there are very few places that don't have to "count their pennies."

PROBLEMS WITH PROGRAM

"Can your wife play the piano?" That was one of the first questions out of the mouth of a board member when their church was interviewing a potential pastor. (My wife, Joyce, addressed that in her book for ministry wives *She Can't Even Play the Piano! Insights for Ministry Wives.*) That question is symbolic of another problem with which small churches wrestle.

The megachurch has a wonderful choir and an orchestra that sounds like a symphony. The smaller church may be blessed to have a teenager who is taking piano, or as I had in Hohenwald, Tennessee, one lonely guitar picker. Should the little church give up because it can't compete? Never!

Not everyone is a fan of the great musical programs that they perceive to be more entertainment than they are worshipful experiences. Let me make it clear: I've been down both sides of this issue. In Wichita I pastored a church with a marvelous music department. Only blocks away were several smaller churches that struggled to find anyone to lead the singing. Did God come only to our great church? You know the answer to that.

There are many tools available to help with music, and I urge you to use them. But more important, multitudes don't really care. My father, to whom I've dedicated this book, represents them. He was tone deaf and knew nothing about music. Often as I stood beside him when we were singing he hit every melody twice—once when he went up through it and again when he came back down. Music was not his thing. Me? I loved music and still do. For Dad, the sooner the music was over, the better for him. He just wanted to hear God's Word. *That* was music to *his* ears. He would have never gone to church for music. He went to be in God's presence. You don't need size to have that. Rather than trying to sing God's presence down, we need to *pray* God's presence down. You may have more people like my dad than you realize. If you do, you're blessed. He was one great lover of God.

PROBLEMS WITH MENTAL BARRIERS

Many churches have a mental battle deciding whether they really want to grow beyond the size with which they've become comfortable. While they may not admit to the problem, some congregations resist growing and raise barriers to keep it from becoming an issue.

Consider this: When the church grows, new people come, people who—

- may take over leadership positions that have all but become sacred family possessions;

- may want to "do" things differently from the way they've always been done;
- may be from a different social or economic group and thereby make the "old-timers" uncomfortable;
- may want to worship in a different style or time frame from the traditional patterns.

And on and on that list could continue. As a result of facing such adjustments, many churches choose to remain small and more "manageable."

In his research project for the Church of the Nazarene, Ken Crow speaks of "conceptual frameworks" and the effect these have on congregational growth.

The conceptual framework "barriers" provides one way to think and discuss the reality that most Protestant congregations don't grow larger than 50 in average attendance and that among larger congregations most do not grow beyond 200. The "200 Barrier" has received more attention, but there appears also to be a "50 Barrier." The concept of "barrier" has proven to be useful in helping churches understand their challenges.

The conceptual framework of "choice-points" provides another way to think and talk about these realities. It appears to be true that at around 50 participants there is a significant choice point for congregations. Particular kinds of fellowship, accountability, and responsibility are possible in churches smaller than about 50. Above that size, other kinds of organizational possibilities and patterns are possible. The choice to grow larger than 50 is not just a matter of overcoming a barrier; it is also a matter of choosing to move from one type of group to a different type.*

We can be sure that God does not want us locked into any

---

*Adapted from <http://www.nazarene.org/itr/papers/
crow_networkcongregations.pdf>.

one size. He will help us break through the "barriers" or "choice-points" that have bound us. He will enable us to become all He has in mind for us—whatever that size may be.

PROBLEMS WITH ACTIVITIES

One more problem that will exist in small churches is activities for different age-groups. The large church will provide many events for children, teens, and adults. We must recognize the attraction of such programs. Children want to be with children, teens with teens, and so on. That's just normal.

So what does the pastor of a smaller church do when there are only one or two in any given age-group? You replace group activities with personal attention. It's very important for children and teens to feel the love of a pastor or Sunday School teacher. The megachurch organizes small-group ministries in order to bring the dynamic of personal attention into the departmental divisions. Smaller churches may not have enough people in various age-groups to have a department or division. But they do have a small group. Practice the dynamics that larger churches are trying to create. You're already there!

Problems? Absolutely! They exist regardless of the size of the church. The pastor whose church is tucked away in the shadow of a tall steeple may sometimes feel overwhelmed. However, remember what Paul said: "I can do everything through him who gives me strength" (Phil. 4:13). Let that be your commitment. *Make the most of what*

Let every difficulty, whether it be a people, finance, or program problem, be turned into an opportunity to lift up Jesus.

you have for His honor and glory. Let every difficulty, whether it be a people, finance, or program problem, be turned into an opportunity to lift up Jesus. And we have the promise in John 12:31—"When I am lifted up . . . [I] will draw all men to myself." Remember after all—the purpose of the church regardless of its size is to lift Him up.

The next time you're tempted to be discouraged and to give up because your church seems so insignificant, remember the story of Jim Cymbala. He was not always the pastor of a major church.

As a matter of fact, Jim did not start out to be a pastor. After suffering an injury at the U.S. Naval Academy that kept him from playing basketball, he went to the University of Rhode Island, where he majored in sociology. In his senior year he met Carol Hutchins, daughter of Rev. Clair Hutchins, who had been his pastor in junior and senior high school. They were married in 1969 and settled down in Brooklyn with jobs in the hectic New York business world.

Pastor Hutchins had been the unofficial overseer of a few small independent churches and suggested to Jim that he supply the pulpit in Newark, New Jersey. While Jim had not had ministerial training, he soon got an education in what it took to be a pastor. Almost before he knew what was happening, he began leading a tiny all-Black church in one of the most difficult mission fields in North America. But that wasn't the end of it. He gives the following account in his wonderful book *Fresh Wind, Fresh Fire*:

> Then one day my father-in-law called from Florida, where he lived, and asked a favor. Would I please go preach four Sunday nights at the multiracial Brooklyn Tabernacle, another church he supervised? Things had hit an all-time low there, he said. I agreed, little suspecting that this step would forever change my life.
>
> The minute I walked in, I could sense that this church

had big problems. The young pastor was discouraged. The meeting began on a hesitant note with just a handful of people. Several more walked in late. The worship style bordered on chaotic; there was little sense of direction. The pastor noticed that a certain man was present—an occasional visitor to the church who sang and accompanied himself on the guitar—and asked him on the spot to come up and render a solo. The man sort of smiled and said no.

"Really, I'm serious." The pastor pleaded. "We'd love to have you sing for us." The man kept resisting. It was terribly awkward. Finally the pastor gave up and continued with congregational singing.

I also remember a woman in the small audience who took it on herself to lead out with a praise chorus, and then jumping into the middle of whatever the pastor was trying to lead.

It was certainly odd, but it wasn't my problem. After all, I was just there to help out temporarily. (The thought that I, at that stage of my development of my ministry, could help anyone showed how desperate things had become.)

I preached and then drove home.

After the second week's service, the pastor stunned me by saying, "I've decided to resign from this church and move out of state. Would you please notify your father-in-law?"

I nodded and said little. When I called that week with the news, the question quickly arose as to whether the church should stay open.

Some years earlier, my mother-in-law had met with other women who were interceding for God to establish a congregation in downtown Brooklyn that would touch people for His glory. That was how this church had actually started—but now all seemed hopeless.

As we discussed what to do, I mentioned something that the pastor had told me. He was sure one of the ushers was helping himself to the offering plate, because the cash never seemed to match the amounts written on people's tithing envelopes. No wonder the church's checking account held less than $10.00.

My father-in-law wasn't ready to give up. "I don't know —I'm not sure God is finished with the place quite yet," he said. "It's a needy part of the city. Let's not throw in the towel too quickly."

"Well, Claire, what are you going to do when the other pastor leaves?" asked his wife, who was listening on their other phone. "I mean, in two weeks . . ."

His voice suddenly brightened. "Jim, how about if you pastor both churches for the time being? Just give it a chance to see if it might turn around?" He wasn't kidding; he really meant it.

I didn't know what to say. One thing I was sure of: I didn't have any magic cure-all for what ailed the Brooklyn Tabernacle. Still, my father-in-law's concern was genuine, so I went along with the plan.

Now, instead of being an amateur in one congregation, I could double my pleasure. For the next year this was my Sunday schedule:

9:00 A.M. Leave home in New Jersey and drive alone to Brooklyn.

10:00 A.M. Conduct the morning service by myself.

11:30 A.M. Race back across Manhattan and through the Holland Tunnel to the Newark Church, where Carol and the others would have already begun the noon service. Preach the sermon.

Late afternoon. Take Carol and the baby to McDonald's, then head back to Brooklyn for the evening service there.

Late evening. Drive back home to New Jersey exhausted and usually discouraged.

Vagrants would wander in occasionally during the meetings in Brooklyn. The attendance dropped to fewer than twenty people, because a number of folks quickly decided I was "too regimented" and elected to go elsewhere.

Sunday mornings without Carol were especially difficult. The pianist had mastered only one chorus, "O How I Love Jesus." We sang it every week, sometimes more than once. All the other selections led to stumbling and discord. This did not seem like a church on the move.

I shall never forget that first Sunday morning offering: $85. The church's monthly mortgage payment was $232, not to mention the utility bills or having anything left over for a pastoral salary.

When the first mortgage payment rolled around at the end of the month, the checking account showed something like $160 in hand. We were going to default right off the bat. How soon would it take to lose the building and be tossed out into the street? That Monday, my day off, I remember praying, "Lord, You have to help me. I don't know much—but I do know that we have to pay this mortgage."

I went to the church on Tuesday. Well, maybe someone will send some money out of the blue, like what happened so often with George Mueller and his orphanage back in England. He just prayed, and the letter or visitor would arrive to meet his need.

The mail came that day—and there was nothing but bills and flyers.

Now I was trapped. I went upstairs, sat at my little desk, put my head down, and began to cry. "God," I sobbed, "What can I do? We can't even pay the mortgage." That night was the midweek service, and I knew there wouldn't be more than three or four people attending. The offering would probably be less than $10. How was I going to get through this?

I called out to the Lord for an hour or so. Eventually, I dried my tears—and a new thought came. Wait a minute!

Besides the mail slot in the front door, the church also has a post office box. I'll go across the street and see what's there. Surely God will answer my prayer!

With renewed confidence I walked across the street, crossed the post office lobby, and twirled the knob on the little box. I peered inside . . . nothing!

As I stepped back into the sunshine, trucks roared down Atlantic Avenue. If one had flattened me just then, I wouldn't have felt any lower. Was God abandoning us? Was I doing something that displeased Him? I trudged wearily back across the street to the little building.

As I unlocked the door, I was met with another surprise. There on the foyer floor was something that hadn't been there just three minutes earlier: a simple white envelope, no address, no stamp—just a white envelope.

With trembling hand I opened it to find—two $50 bills.

I began shouting all by myself in the empty church. "God, You came through! You came through!" We had $160 in the bank, and with this $100 we could make the mortgage payment. My soul let out a deep Hallelujah. What a lesson for a young pastor!

To this day I don't know where that money came from. I only know it was a sign to me that God was near and faithful (13-17).*

Jim Cymbala went on, by God's grace and strength, to build the great Brooklyn Tabernacle. This congregation has become one of the most influential churches in America. But it began in the shadow of the great steeples in New York City. And it experienced all the problems that any church can have. It's a great example of the fact that God did not put you in the shadow to let you die or just merely exist. *He has put you where you*

*Taken from *Fresh Wind, Fresh Fire,* by Jim Cymbala; Dean Merrill. Copyright © 1997 by Jim Cymbala. Used by permission of The Zondervan Corporation.

are because He believes in you. So believe in yourself and enjoy His will.

Your church may never become a megachurch like the Brooklyn Tabernacle. In fact, your church probably won't. Does that mean you're a failure? No—never! I've related this story to illustrate the fact that all churches have problems. The assignment of every pastor in every church is not to become big. It's to become faithful regardless of the problems and difficulties he or she may encounter.

I encourage you to join Paul in his testimony of confidence he shared in Phil. 4:13: "I can do everything through him who gives me strength."

POINTS TO PONDER

1. Every church has problems of some kind. How does it help you to realize this?
2. Consider: If the church is a battleground rather than a sanctuary, very few new people will ever show up. How can you face this option?
3. Realize: The bigger your church is, the larger the problems may be.
4. Everywhere people are, problems will be found. How does it help the pastor of a small church to realize this?

Scripture

I have told you these things so that in me you may have peace. In the world you will have trouble. But take heart! I have overcome the world (John 16:33).

Prayer

Dear Father, thank You for Your gift of strength and peace for the task You've set before me. Please help me to be a peacemaker. I want to face any problems that come my way in the confidence of Your grace. In Jesus' name I pray. Amen.

4
PLEASURE

**There's pleasure to be found in the
shadow of the steeple.**

"Pastor, I knew you'd come." With those warm words Bill defined the reason that I was out in the bean fields of south Florida at 1:30 A.M. He was a farmer and was facing the potential disaster of his crop freezing in the cold weather. I could have stayed in my warm bed as my wife had encouraged me to do. None of my professors at seminary had taught me how to make coffee to take into the fields to farmers on a cold winter night. In fact, I don't recall that anyone ever told me I should make pastoral calls at 1:30 in the morning. So why was I out there? Because I enjoyed being close to my people—especially when they were in need. There's great pleasure to be experienced when you help your people get through a tough situation.

What a wonderful way to live! I agree 100 percent with H. B. London Jr. and Neil B. Wiseman, who wrote in their book *The Heart of a Great Pastor,* "No occupational fulfillment in the whole world faintly compares with the satisfaction a pastor enjoys who loves God, loves his call, and shows love for the people he serves" (120). They also ask, "Why should ministry be viewed as anything less than an adventuresome way to live? Why do so many contemporary pastors sigh for something that might allow them to respectably leave pastoral service?" That's a question for which I've never discovered the answer. It's an incredible compliment when God says, "I believe in you so much that I'm going to entrust to your care some of the people for whom I died." This compliment is only magnified when He

says, "I have a difficult assignment, but together we can do it."
What a wonderful way to live!

One of the blessings of pastoring a small church is the pleasure of getting to be close to the people. That rural church in south Florida was not the smallest of those around, but it was only a fraction of the size of the huge churches located just up the road in Miami. The people could have driven up there if they had wanted to be part of the big scene. They chose not to do that. Those farmers loved the family atmosphere we had.

That bitter cold night in the bean fields was richly rewarding. To see Bill's eyes light up when he spotted me with that big steaming coffeepot let me know that I had done the right thing.

Pastors of smaller churches have the opportunity to get closely involved in the lives of their people. Admittedly, this is not for everyone. Some pastors aren't people-oriented. Frankly, I don't understand that, but I know it's true. I'm a people person who found great pleasure in being close to my congregation. I was richly rewarded as I watched the young people of that church respond to God's call on their lives. And I'm still clipping pleasure coupons as I watch them develop as pastors, pastors' spouses, teachers, and very strong laypersons.

Do pastors of the giant churches experience this same joy? A few, but very few. Between the large-church pastors and their young people is a network of individuals. I know of no "senior" pastor of a large church who can do what Pastor Lyle is doing. Lyle is taking a class I'm teaching for a nearby college. He pastors a small church, fewer than 25 in attendance. Last night I watched his eyes light up as he described what happened last Sunday in the Sunday School class he teaches. His class of three teenagers had enjoyed a wonderful time in God's presence. He's making a difference in the lives of those young people who would not be in church except for his care. As they grow in grace, Lyle will enjoy the pleasure of knowing he has made a difference.

I repeat—one of the greatest pleasures of pastoring small churches in the shadow of the megachurch is that of being able to be closely involved in your people's lives. In his book *Effective Small Churches in the Twenty-First Century* Carl Dudley states,

> For most small church pastors, the satisfactions are overwhelmingly in the area of personal relationships. Typical satisfactions include working with people, sharing lives and crises, feeling loved and supported, preaching and pastoral calls, ministering to people, having a family and sharing family with others, and enabling people (79).

While it's true that you can't "eat" pleasure—many small-church pastors are poorly paid—neither can you buy pleasure. One of the most priceless things a person can ever experience is readily available to the small-church pastor. I could never have bought the enjoyment I experienced as the result of my activities one Sunday morning in the shadow of some big steeples in Nashville.

"Pastor, we can't go to church today. The kids don't have any shoes. But I did some ironing for a neighbor yesterday, and here's my tithe." And with that statement, this mother of three dropped six dimes into my hand. They felt like pure gold. Sixty cents may not be much money, but on that Sunday morning in 1952 it seemed nothing less than a fortune.

That tiny church in Nashville was my second pastorate. We met in a house where we

One of the greatest pleasures of pastoring small churches in the shadow of the megachurch is that of being able to be closely involved in your people's lives.

had removed some walls in order to have a room large enough to worship together. In case you don't know it, Nashville has always had megachurches. Still, there is and always has been a place for the smaller, more family-oriented church. So that little congregation in the Vine Hill section of town had a place in the Kingdom. There were people in that little church who would never even attempt to attend one of the large, beautiful worship centers.

I had gone to pick up that little family to give them a ride to church. They would have felt totally out of place in a large church. They lived close enough to walk to the big church down the street but would not have felt comfortable in that more formal, less personal atmosphere.

As pastor of this church of fewer than 50, I had close contact with every member. It was as though I had become part of their family. Whatever happened in their lives, good or bad, I was aware of it. And the people loved me. The material rewards were few, but the emotional and spiritual returns were enormous. That week when I was able to make sure those children got shoes, I felt like the most important man in the world.

By pure necessity pastors of large churches are somewhat distanced from some of their people. The demands on those pastors never seem to end. Between the committees and boards on which they are asked to serve are always meetings to attend. Add to that the requests for your attendance at conferences and seminars, and there's very little time left to just interact with the people. Many senior pastors at large churches become preaching pastors and have little interaction with their people.

I've lost count of the times while pastoring a large church that I was left out of family experiences in which I would have really enjoyed participating. More often than not, I was left out because "Pastor, we know how busy you are."

That never happened in that smaller church in south Florida. We were adopted into every family and shared in their celebrations and times together.

The pleasure of pastoring in a smaller church often catches us by surprise. At least I know that Pastor David was surprised at what happened to him. Although his church is not that small, it still could be hidden in the shadows of some of the churches in his town. His congregation is in an older section of town and is difficult to get to from outside that area. There's been some pressure to relocate, but that would mean abandoning an inner-city neighborhood where a lot of blue-collar, hardworking people live. So led by a kind, loving pastor, the church has stayed there. They're in fact trying to take good care of their neighbors by opening their facilities during the week. They provide childcare opportunities and reach out to the surrounding area.

One member of Pastor David's small flock wanted to express the love the congregation felt toward him. So one Sunday he arranged for everyone in the sanctuary to have a beautiful rose. On signal, they all came to the front one at a time to present their rose to the pastor and his wife as an expression of their love. The man who told me about that experience said it was the greatest outpouring of love he had ever seen.

I happen to know Pastor David, and he says, "That was one of the highlights of my life." This would not have happened in a huge church. There are some experiences that are best enjoyed in the confines of a family.

My son-in-law, Randy, is an emergency room physician and is on the frontline of helping people in dire need. From his experiences of the past 17 years, he's written a great story in my book *Real Men, Real Faith.*

Being in the emergency room means working all hours of the day and night. Sometimes it means working on Christmas, Thanksgiving, and other special days. It means missing a lot of family fun. It also means dealing with some unsavory characters at times. Randy has been yelled at and cursed at—and all the other things that angry people do when they're really hurting. Most of the patients he helps never say thank you. If they have

There's something very rewarding in realizing that you made a difference in someone's life.

anything to say, it's a complaint about how long they had to wait or to ask why they're not feeling much better when they leave.

So why do guys like Randy subject themselves to such situations? It is not for the money. They could make a lot more in a more traditional field of medicine. Doctors like Randy are like many pastors I know who find pleasure in helping people. *There's something very rewarding in realizing that you made a difference in someone's life.* Occasionally someone takes the time to tell you about the impact you've had on his or her life. When that happens, the joy we feel is priceless.

One day I was playing golf with a new acquaintance and we were talking about our families. When he discovered that Randy was my son-in-law, he became excited and quite emotional. "Could you please give him a message from me?" "Sure!" I answered. He went on to explain that his wife had experienced a heart attack in the middle of the night. He carried her to the car and rushed her to the hospital where Randy was on duty. My new friend was ecstatic with praise for the man who, in his own words, had saved his wife's life. He wanted me to be sure to tell "Dr. Randy" how grateful they were.

Later at a family gathering I expressed that man's strong words of appreciation to Randy. His eyes lit up, and a smile went from ear to ear. That's why he works the long, weary hours. He receives great pleasure from helping people.

In his book *They Call Me Pastor* H. B. London Jr. explains where some pastors find great pleasure. The size of the church is immaterial.

I grew to love the title [pastor] and to this day respond to it with joy. It made me feel special when they called me pastor. Pastor,

. . . Thanks for the sermon.

. . . I need to talk to you.

. . . My mom just died.

. . . We're going to have a baby.

. . . God seems to be directing us to another church.

. . . I believe God has called me into the ministry. How can I know for sure?

. . . The X-rays do not look good. Could you pray with me?

. . . We will be moving to the East Coast next week. We will miss you.

. . . When do you think you will have time to get a haircut?

. . . I'm gay—what should I do?

. . . My wife just left me.

. . . Our daughter is pregnant.

. . . Thanks for being there when I needed you.

The list is endless, but you know what I mean and how it feels (11).

There's no doubt in my mind that small-church pastors are closer to their people than megachurch pastors. This means that the intensity of their pleasure in pastoring many times exceeds that of the pastor of the huge church, who is several layers removed from close personal relationship with the people.

So what are the prospects for a pastor to find pleasure in pastoring the church nestled in the shadow of a huge steeple? They're very good as he or she focuses on winning people to Jesus by lifting Him up. This is the chief goal and purpose of all churches regardless of their sizes.

In his book *Effective Small Churches*, Carl Dudley makes some strong, clear statements about the special relationships that exist between the pastor and the people in a small church. Although members of small congregations want the benefit of skilled pastors to serve their churches, they place an even higher priority on having a pastor whom they feel they know personally. Later he writes, "The church wants a lover." He adds,

Members of small churches have a curious method of re-emphasizing the common humanity of the pastor. They enjoy his or her mistakes. They tell stories about the time when the pastor stumbled into the pulpit, or made a slip of the tongue in preaching, or announced the wrong name in the midst of the funeral, or dropped the ring at the wedding, ad nauseam. To the educated pastor who prides himself or herself on polished skills of ministry, these memories are humiliating. To the members the stories underscore what they find most appealing about the pastor; he or she is a real person. The stories are intended not to criticize, but to bind pastor to people (80-81).

Take it from one who has been there and made those blunders. If it were not for the special relationships that exist between pastor and people, those mistakes would have become major disasters.

As I already stated, I'm currently teaching a class of small-church pastors. This is under the auspices of Barclay College, in Haviland, Kansas. All my students pastor churches of 30 or fewer, and most of them are bivocational. I asked them to write a short paper about what they would miss if they moved to a large church. My heart was touched when I read this expression of joy from one of them:

I actually have a dream of pastoring a large church some day. I see the challenge of having multiple programs and ministries in a wonderful light. In the church that I pastor, I would like to see someone coming to the Lord at least a couple of times a month. I often see a vision of a full choir and two services on Sunday morning. Weekday evenings would be filled, not with my presence, but with the presence of church members leading children in Bible studies, helping young people deal with current difficult issues and personal problems, and adults coming together to worship and pray for the work of the church.

However, there are definite drawbacks to that large-church picture. I think what I would miss would be getting to know every member on a personal level. Sometimes knowing people this way can be difficult, because it can allow for a certain type of familiarity that breeds contempt, as someone has said. People who gain this type of familiarity do not take criticism well or will often feel that there has been serious harm in the personal relationship. If the relationship is genuine, this is rarely a problem.

I would miss the family feel of the all-church potluck, shared cleanup days, and ministry work done side by side. The small church offers so much in building personal relationships and helping people one-on-one that cannot be easily accomplished by the pastor of a large church. In the smaller setting the pastor is able to fulfill this role. Though the toll can be heavy personally, I feel God does call us to become involved in the lives of our people. That involvement is to be sacrificial just as Jesus' sacrifice for us was sacrificial. The example of the Lord as He walked the earth teaching His small band of 12 and the multitudes that followed Him showed how He became personally involved in their lives. In most cases the pastor of a small church feels that strong personal involvement with the people more so than the large church pastor.

This is one small-church pastor who has found genuine pleasure in the assignment the Lord has given to him, even though he serves in the shadow of a giant steeple. You, too, may have that wonderful experience if you'll make the most of the opportunity the Lord has given to you.

So, dear pastor, although you may not have a large crowd, you have the wonderful opportunity to experience great joy and close connection with the lives of your people. I want to remind you that although you may be pastoring in the shadow of a tall steeple, you're in a unique relationship with your people. Prepare your mind and heart to enjoy the special pleasures God has prepared for you.

In his book *How to Thrive as a Small Church Pastor,* Steve Bierly issues a great challenge.

Why do we automatically assume that the large congregation with the brand-new building, the cutting-edge pastor, and the seven-days-a-week ministries is the place where God is really at work? Our tendency to jump to this conclusion has more to do with the fact that we live with success-oriented, "bigger is better," entrepreneurial America than it does with our being Bible-believing Christians.

It seems clear from a study of Revelation that Jesus is concerned with congregations learning to love Him and their members, making the most of whatever limited resources they have, hanging on and being faithful in tough times, learning what it means to live holy lives, and depending utterly on Christ—not their strength—for power, opportunity, and prosperity. Aren't these also the concerns of small churches that are seeking to follow Christ? As a small church pastor, aren't you actually spending a lot of your time, preaching, teaching, and working on areas that are vitally important to Christ? Doesn't Christ's agenda fit better with the "traditional" pastor role so many small congregations expect the clergy to fill than with the CEO models advocated today? Could it be that Jesus is actually pleased with you and is blessing, or will bless, your ministry even though no national magazine will ever cite you as one of the "ten most important pastors of the year"? (151).

Could it be that Jesus is actually pleased with *you?* That, pastor friend, is the greatest realization any of us can ever experience, of hearing the Heavenly Father say, "Well done." This should produce a deep sense of well-being and encourage us to make the most of our opportunity regardless of whatever situation He may call us to serve in.

POINTS TO PONDER

1. What's the greatest pleasure enjoyed by the pastor of a small church?
2. Do you find pleasure in the assignment God has given to you? If not, why not?
3. Have you experienced the joy of making a difference in someone's life? If not, make this priority one.
4. Have you thought this through: Can it be that Jesus is pleased with me? Is there a reason for Him to be?

Scripture

Delight yourself in the LORD *and he will give you the desires of your heart* (Ps. 37:4).

Prayer

Dear Father, thank You for trusting and believing in me. I love Your presence in my heart and Your will for my life. I find great delight in carrying out Your will. Thank You for the privilege of serving You. In Your Son's name I pray. Amen.

5
PROSPECTS

**There are great prospects in the
shadow of the steeple.**

"We want to be part of bringing new life to the northwest side
of town. And we believe that God wants to use us to reach the
people in this area for Him." So with that purpose and God's
calling on their lives, Pastor Mark took his family, along with a
group of very sharp young adults and their families, and set out
on a mission.

I thought about pointing out to them that there was a very
large established church in their neighborhood, which just recently built a multimillion-dollar building that has all of the
amenities anyone could ever want in a church. The pastor is
very popular and has been in the area for over 35 years. So why
would you plant a new church there? Why would you deliberately locate in the shadow of such a large steeple with the in-
tention of starting a baby church?

Fortunately, I did not make those discouraging remarks. As
I've already stated, even though it may seem as though everyone is pulling into the parking lot Sunday mornings at that
large church, the fact remains that the majority (well over 50
percent) of the people in the area are not attending church
anywhere. So that small group of committed laypeople have attached themselves to a very wonderful young pastor and en-
tered a field that's still white unto harvest. Yes, the megachurch
is reaching a multitude, but they're not close to reaping all the
harvest in that field. This group believes God wants them to

reach the people who are not attending the big church. Does He? You know the answer!

At present this little congregation does not even have a church building in which they can meet for worship. So they're meeting in a local school. This excited small group of 30 or so left a thriving church. They were respected, involved, and comfortable in that large congregation that has a great influence on their city. They've taken on an assignment in the densely populated residential area that already has several strong churches in addition to the megachurch. Initially, some might wonder if they have any idea what they're facing.

The majority of unchurched people who learn of God's love will do so in the smaller church setting.

While we may wonder if they're wasting their efforts, don't forget the Risen Lamb Church in Kansas City. They started from scratch—but with a mission to reach unchurched people for whom Jesus died. One year later they numbered 250. However, if there had been only 50, it still would have been worth the effort. *If Jesus loved the people of that urban neighborhood enough to die for them, then whoever gets the message to them must be pleasing to God.*

Will the group that's just starting out in Wichita, Kansas, have the same results? That remains to be seen. However, one thing is sure. They'll reach people for Jesus who would not have ever known about His love for them. Megachurches are not for everyone, as we've already noted. The majority of unchurched people who learn of God's love will do so in the smaller church setting.

In his research paper* for the Department of Church

---

* <www.nazarene.org/itr/papers/crow_networkcongregations.pdf>

Growth, Church of the Nazarene, Ken Crow quotes Carl Dudley: "'The small church is not an organization; it is an association that generates and lives by its social capital.' Therefore, 'small churches are not organizational errors to be corrected [as some might assume], but intentional choices of members who put a priority on human relationships.'"

He points out further that "particular kinds of fellowship, accountability, and responsibility are possible in churches smaller than about fifty." In the fully alive small church, personal relationships are very strong. It's very difficult to be an anonymous worshiper there. Because of this intimacy, the prospects for the small church to reach new people for Jesus are wonderful. We must understand that the small church does not set out to stay small. To do so would surely relegate that group to being a "country club of saints." Surely we don't want to fall into the trap of smallness for smallness's sake. We must reach out to those who don't know Jesus and are turned off by the megachurch.

What makes the prospects so good? Again, I turn to Ken Crow's report, where he quotes Tom Peters: "There's some marvelous anthropological research that . . . says one hundred and fifty-three people, to be precise, is the maximum size unit to really get things done in an energetic fashion."

The realization that large churches accommodate that fact by incorporating the use of small groups for ministry should encourage the small-church pastor. He already has a small-group ministry. In fact, most (remember that over half of all North American churches average less than 50 in attendance) have some room to grow before needing to be concerned about small groups.

People are looking for a place where they can be something other than a number. They'll respond to the personal touch that's more available in the small congregation.

Again, I want to emphasize that we must not limit what God

wants to do. He may very well take a mustard seed and turn it into a giant tree, as Jesus referred to in Matt. 13:31-32:

The kingdom of heaven is like a mustard seed, which a man took and planted in his field. Though it is the smallest of all your seeds, yet when it grows, it is the largest of garden plants and becomes a tree, so that the birds of the air come and perch in its branches.

That's basically what happened at Saddleback Church in Lake Forest, California. Pastor Rick Warren and his wife, Kay, began this congregation in their home in 1980 with seven people. With a deep desire to impact their community, the church has grown to more than 22,000 people in weekly attendance. That is some large mustard seed tree!

So what are the prospects for the church nestled in the shadow of a great steeple? They're the same as those of the megachurch—winning people to Jesus.

God might want to take a church that's ministering in a difficult situation and keep it strong and productive even if it never becomes large. *The greatest prospect any church has is to be the best it can be to the glory of God.* Still, I'm haunted by John Vaughan's discovery in his research on church growth in North American that 80 percent of the churches have reached a plateau or are declining. *In other words, they have become victims to the curse of barrenness.*

I'm writing these lines during the summer Olympics in Athens, Greece. The size difference between the athletes is tremendous. Some are in the 6'5", 300-pound class. And there are other athletes in the 4'10", 80-pound class. Which is best? You may say, "That's a silly question. Obviously it depends on the Olympic event." This analogy applies to the basic truth with which we're dealing in churches.

Those 300-pound athletes can't do what the 80-pound gymnasts can accomplish. Imagine the big discus-thrower trying to do the high bar or the balance beam. Now that would be a comical sight! On that same note, try to picture the tiny 80-pound gymnast trying to throw the discus or the 16-pound shot. Ridiculous, isn't it? We understand that each one of them is equipped to excel in his or her event. He or she is not expected to match the performance of those in other categories.

So it is with churches. The pastors of small churches should not, must not, feel less used by God than the large-church pastor any more than a gymnast feel less a part of the Olympics than the discus-thrower. Respect is given to the accomplishment of each of them in his or her own field of assignment.

At the Olympics what matters is to win the gold medal, which incidentally is the same size regardless of the size of the athlete. *The "gold medal" placed on the neck of the pastor who faithfully pursues his or her assignment and lifts up Jesus is the same regardless of the size of the church.* There's no "mega-gold" and "mini-gold." There's only one size.

The prospects for personal joy and the internal rewards of knowing you have helped to build God's kingdom are wonderful. You may be like the 80-pound gymnast, but your outlook and prospects for gold are the same as that of the physical giant.

Pastors should be encouraged with the prospects for their church even though on any given Sunday morning their flock is overshadowed by the crowd down the street. In his book *Effective Small Churches in the Twenty-First Century* Carl Dudley points out the following:

The "gold medal" placed on the neck of the pastor who faithfully pursues his or her assignment and lifts up Jesus is the same regardless of the size of the church.

Small churches will continue to be the quiet majority of Protestant congregations. . . .

Two organizational changes early in the 20th Century have affected the small church. First, small churches have seen the rise and decline of denominational structures that organized resources, developed programs, projected strategies, and claimed the allegiance of the participating congregations. Small churches, once nurtured through networks of personal relationships, had to learn how to work with organizational committees and staff. Second, a few congregations that have grown into very large megachurches dominate the media landscape. These large congregations —typically located in the suburbs near an arterial highway—have eclipsed the old first church that once was the denominational flagship at the center of the larger cities or towns in the area.

Despite the dominating shadow of megachurches, they represent less than 1 percent of congregations in the United States. The vast majority of congregations desire a more modest goal—to have a full program of worship, education, and fellowship based on their own financial resources and to be served by at least one professionally trained, full-time pastor as a generalist (not a specialist) who could meet the wide range of congregational needs (27).

Please note two strong points that Dudley makes:

1. History is on the side of the small church.
2. The vast majority of congregations simply want a full program of church activities and a pastor who can meet a wide range of congregational needs.

This means that the prospects of the smaller church are excellent. Again, I want to point out that we must never be satisfied with "barrenness." "Small but pure" is not a status to be pursued. It would be far better to pursue "small but growing by the grace of God."

Tragically, many churches are satisfied to survive even though the fields are still "ripe unto harvest" (John 4:35). Tom Rainer points out the following in his book *Giant Awakenings:*

> In the last quarter of a century our nation has become a mission field as a growing percentage of our population dropped out of church involvement. One of the consequences of this trajectory is that as many as 85% of all churches in America are either plateaued or declining. In 1988, church growth expert Win Arn declared that 71% of the U.S. population are either unaffiliated with any religion or are Christians in "name only." George Gallup's study in the same year showed that 44% of the population is solidly unchurched (141).

Rainer had stated earlier, "Americans who moved to the smaller communities did so for affordable housing, a better quality of life, and a less frantic pace. Smaller churches will attract many of these wearied people who desire a simpler, more intimate lifestyle" (7).

The prospects for the future growth of the smaller church are wonderful if there is a vision to reach people with the message of the gospel. It's time we looked at the "field of souls" like a farmer viewing his or her fields at harvest. Time is of the essence. The longer we wait, the more of the harvest we'll miss. In the Introduction I mentioned the Kansas wheat harvest. I've seen the combines running well into the blackness of the night. When the harvest is ripe, hope runs high and nothing prevents the farmer from cutting his or her wheat. And the approach is the same whether the farmer has 300 or 3,000 acres. Get the harvest in before a storm comes and ruins it.

In his illuminating work *Surprising Insights from the Unchurched,* Tom Rainer points out the following:

> Only 41% of Americans attend church services on a typical weekend. Each new generation becomes increasingly unchurched. Slightly over one-half (51%) of the builder

generation (born before 1946) attends church on a typical weekend. But only 41% of the boomers (born between 1946-1964) and 34% of the busters (born between 1965-1976) attend church on a given weekend.

Our recent research on the younger generation, the bridgers (born 1977-1994) indicates that only 4% of the teenagers understand the gospel and have accepted Christ even if they attend church (33).

They're out there. They're prospects for the Kingdom. We must not let the fact that we're "small farmers" keep us from reaching those our Father has placed in our harvest field.

So regardless of the size of your church, I encourage you to, as Paul wrote in Philippians, "Press on toward the goal to win the prize to which God has called me heavenward in Christ Jesus" (Phil. 3:14). Be assured, pastor—there are great prospects for your church—even in the shadow of the steeple.

POINTS TO PONDER

1. Consider: Since over 50 percent of the people in any area are not attending church anywhere, what are the prospects for your church?
2. Realize: People are anxious for personal relationships. This means that prospects for the small church are very good. How will you capitalize on this?
3. Consider: "The gold medal placed on the neck of a pastor who faithfully pursues his or her assignment and lifts up Jesus is the same regardless of the size of the church."
4. The vast majority of congregations have a very modest goal. What should this say to any small-church pastor?

Scripture

Do you not say, "Four months more and then the harvest?" I tell you, open your eyes and look at the fields! They are ripe for harvest (John 4:35).

Prayer

Dear Father, Open my eyes so that I can see what You see. You have placed me in the midst of a field of souls for whom You died. Give me the will and the wisdom to reach them for You. In Jesus' name I pray. Amen.

6
PRIDE

**Taking pride in our assignment—
even in the shadow of the steeple**

I've heard it—you've heard it. The statement begins with the words, "I'm just a . . ." and you can fill in that blank with a multitude of statements that show a lack of pride. I know we preach against carnal pride that causes us to puff up and think we're better than someone else—and sometimes *everyone* else. That's not what I'm addressing. I'm calling for righteous self-respect that rightfully belongs to every child of the King.

This feeling of pride is the possession of all of us who have been rescued from the havoc of sin and are now designated as the children of God. Every child of the King is valuable.

So there's no such thing as "just a layperson" or "just the pastor of a small church." *There are no small assignments in the kingdom of God.* Every assignment is so important that God has chosen special people to carry it out. In Eph. 4:11-12 Paul did not elevate one position above another when he said, "It was he who gave some to be apostles, some to be prophets, some to be evangelists, and some to be pastors and teachers." Note their ultimate assignment. "To prepare God's people for works of service, so that the body of Christ may be built up."

Which is the most important assignment? That's right! They're all equally designated by God.

So suppose we paraphrase that verse to read, "It was He who gave some to pastor megachurches, some to pastor large churches, some to pastor medium-sized churches, and some to

If God has called you to pastor a small church, take pride in the fact that God believes in you.

pastor small churches." For what? "To reach people with the message of His love and to prepare them for service to build up the kingdom of God." Again I ask, which assignment is most important? The obvious answer is—neither! Any calling of God is as important in His eyes as any other. So if He has called you to pastor a small church, take pride in the fact that God believes in you.

I can honestly say that the small assignments I've experienced were richly rewarding. In fact, at the time I was carrying out those callings I felt as rewarded as I did later when carrying out a very large assignment.

The key to experiencing pride in each of our assignments is to clearly understand why we do what we do. What is our purpose?

In my book *Real Men—Real Faith*, Rob Taylor illustrates how we can take pride in our assignment whatever that might be. While playing high school football in Ohio, he was named an all-state lineman. Rob was recruited by several Big Ten Conference schools that had winning programs. He ended up going to Northwestern University, which had one of the worst records in the nation. Nothing changed when Rob joined the team. During his four years, the Northwestern University Wildcats football team was 1-41-1. That's awful!

After graduating from college, he was associated with three professional football teams before ending up with the Tampa Bay Buccaneers expansion team. You guessed it! He was hooked up with another losing team. In fact, he spent eight years losing.

I asked Rob, "How in the world did you handle losing all of

the time? How did you emotionally handle never winning?" I'll never forget his answer. He explained that when he was 12 years old, he committed himself to be an athlete for Jesus. His father had taken him to a Billy Graham crusade in Dallas. After the service one night, he met Coach Tom Landry and all-pro quarterback Roger Staubach. It was then that Rob felt God's call on his life.

All of those years while he was playing football for losing teams, Rob Taylor was doing his best for Jesus. In fact, he told me, "I never looked at the scoreboard. I was an offensive lineman, and if I carried out my assignment and made my blocks, I knew that Jesus was pleased." I felt like shouting! Here was a man who had learned to have pride even in a bad situation. He was playing for an audience of One.

Before you say, "Jesus doesn't care about football," remember it really wasn't about football. In the clearest analysis, it was about Paul's admonition in Col. 3:23—"Whatever you do, work at it with all your heart, as working for the Lord, not for men." Rob was not playing football for men. He was using football to glorify God.

Why do you do what you do? You should be doing it for Jesus. Make your block, carry out your assignment, and then you can take pride in your faithfulness whether you're on a championship team or a losing team. Or as we're considering, carry out your assignment so that whether you're pastoring a maxichurch or a minichurch, you can take pride in doing well what God has called you to do.

I've been blessed to have been associated with people who influenced my attitude without being conscious that they were doing so. While I was a student at Trevecca Nazarene University in Nashville in the early 1950s, A. B. Mackey was the president. I don't remember the occasion, but I do remember the sparkle in Dr. Mackey's eyes and the excitement in his voice when he made a statement I've never forgotten: "If I was a ditch digger, I would want to dig the straightest, finest ditches I could dig for Jesus." Take pride in digging ditches? Absolutely! Whatever we do, we must do the very best we can for the glory of God.

Charles Spurgeon was one of the most powerful and productive preachers of the 19th century. Because of his success at New Park Street Chapel in London, young men began to ask him to teach them. So he started Pastors' College. By 1891, 845 persons had been trained in that school. In 1865 he began an annual conference for students and graduates of Pastors' College. Spurgeon delivered 27 addresses to the conference, of which 12 were compiled into a book titled *An All-Round Ministry*. Pride in one's assignment from God was extremely important to these people. In an effort to instill a sense of pride in their calling regardless of the size of their congregation, Spurgeon said, "If God had made you a house cricket and bidden you chirp, you could not do better than fulfill His will" (72).

In a powerful illustration of taking pride in the assignment God has given, he stated,

There is not only a work ordained for each man, but each man is fitted for his work. Men are not cast in molds by the thousands; we are each one distinct from his fellow. When each of us was made, the mold was broken;—a very satisfactory circumstance in the case of some men, and I greatly question whether it is not an advantage in the case of us all. If we are, however, vessels for the Master's use, we ought to have no choice about what that vessel may be. There was a cup which stood upon the communion table when our Lord ate that Passover which He had so desired to eat with His disciples before He suffered; and, assuredly, that cup was honored when it was put to His lips and then passed to the apostles. Who would not be like that cup? But there was a basin also which the Master took into which He poured water and washed the disciples' feet. I protest that I have no choice whether to be the chalice or the basin. Fain would I be whichever the Lord wills so long as He will but use me. But this is plain—the cup would have made a very insufficient basin, and the basin would have been a very improper cup for the communion feast. So you, my brother, may be the cup, and I will be the basin; but let the cup be a cup and the basin a basin and each one of us just what he is fitted to be (73).

If we let the megachurch represent the chalice and the small church the basin, we understand our calling is to be used by God for His purpose. When that happens, we can take pride in however the Master uses us.

Where pride is concerned, there is danger in going to either extreme. Too much pride is as wrong as too little. While the large-church pastor will need to be on guard against too much pride, the small-church pastor *must* guard against feeling sorry for himself or herself because of his or her assignment. Again, there are no small assignments in the Kingdom.

Failure to have pride in the assignment God has given you is wrong. You've heard it said, "God don't make no junk." We use that grammatically incorrect colloquialism to encourage children to realize they have great value to God. I want to restate that. "God don't give no junk assignments!" Every opportunity He gives to us is important to His kingdom.

To approach this important point from another perspective, take note that pastoring a smaller church and leading it to be a strong small church is a major accomplishment. Small-church pastors must be more versatile than the megachurch pastor who has a staff of specialists working with him or her. It takes special grace to pastor in small, difficult places.

It takes special grace to pastor in small, difficult places.

In one church I pastored I was the only staff member. I was not only senior pastor but also youth director, bus driver, choir director (and I can't even read music!), custodian, and so on. My wife taught our largest Sunday school class, was missionary president, and learned to play the organ so she could cover up my lack of musical talent.

It was hard work. But when things began to "click," we were proud of the results that God was bringing about through us. I'm convinced that God assigned a regiment of angels to help us so that we wouldn't embarrass the Kingdom. I was there under divine appointment, and what He calls us to do He enables us to do. I loved what I was doing.

I still look back with pride on the 10 years I spent in that assignment. The church grew steadily, but just as important, I grew. I was proud of what He was helping us to accomplish. The young people were infected with love for Jesus and responded positively when God invited them to join His team. They saw pastoring in a positive light. You won't be surprised when I tell you that those whom God called into the ministry have also tackled some very difficult situations.

One of those young people, Mary, married Dale, a young man she met at a Christian college, who was called to pastor and was gratified at having been chosen by God. Together they accepted a difficult assignment in a major city in the South. Talk about pastoring in the shadow of the steeple, how about being in the shadow of more than a dozen large steeples? The greater Atlanta area has multiple huge steeples.

The church Dale and Mary pastor was in a giant free fall when they arrived. Attendance had once been 250. At the time they went there, the church was running about 80. The people were discouraged, defeated, and all but ready to give up. When Pastor Dale and Mary moved into that losing situation, you might think he would have wondered why God had "committed" them to such a negative situation. Not that couple! They had proven themselves to be worthy of God's trust. The first three churches they had pastored each had 19 people when Dale and Mary arrived. Dale told me that he thought they had gotten stuck in a "19 rut." However, pastoring those challenging situations had strengthened their resolve to serve God faithfully. It had also matured them so that trouble spots did not defeat them.

So when they arrived in Atlanta and began to pastor those 80 discouraged people, their first job was to change the atmosphere. They were determined that their church would not cater to "down-in-the-mouth losers." They would take pride in who they were and their privilege to serve God. Pastor Dale and Mary infected that congregation with a sense of pride. And just for the record, every pastor is an attitude carrier. He or she either infects the congregation with pride in their assignment or with pity for what God is asking them to do.

How do you take 80 discouraged people and turn them into 300 aggressive believers? *You get their eyes off their poverty and onto the riches of God's grace.* Begin to reach outside your circle of safety. You minister to a struggling neighborhood and hurting people in your community. Then, of all things, as you gain strength, you decide to plant a new church with 50 of your people.

Every pastor is an attitude carrier. He or she either infects the congregation with pride in their assignment or with pity for what God is asking them to do.

As I talked with Pastor Dale, I was tempted to say, "You'll never reach 5,000 with that attitude." I didn't tell him that, because I know what he would have said: "God didn't call us to build a church of 5,000 or even 500. He called us to be faithful. Whatever the result is, that's up to Him." Dale's pride is not in the size of his church. Rather, it's in hearing God say, "Well done, thou good and faithful servant" (Matt. 25:21, KJV).

In the shadow of the steeple is an assignment that will result in a healthy feeling of pride. You may never be recognized by your denominational leaders or any other group. In fact, you most likely will not receive special recognition. And you may very well wonder if anyone knows how hard your assignment might be.

Someone *does* know. God placed you where you are, and wherever He puts you is where He focuses His eyes. So take pride in doing what you do for Jesus. You may very well want to do what Rob Taylor has done and "play for an audience of One." Then you can rejoice in winning your assignment for Him regardless of the numbers on the scoreboard.

One more truth in this area is critical for us to examine. In his book *Shepherding the Small Church* Glenn Daman quotes David Ray. "The dominating and most debilitating problem in a high percentage of small churches is low self-esteem, resulting in low morale" (221). *Your attitude, whatever that might be, will infect your congregation.* Pride in God's assignment can be an uplifting force to your congregation.

Yes, there are times in all our lives when we feel defeated even as Elijah did in 1 Kings 19:4 as he sat alone in the desert under a broom tree. "I've had enough, Lord," he said. "Take my life. I'm no better than my ancestors." The Lord was not pleased with that attitude and arranged a renewal experience for Elijah. He gave him a personal encounter while he was still having his "pity party."

Neither is God happy when we succumb to such feelings today. God does not want His people to feel sorry for themselves. And, pastor, I repeat—you're the key to their attitude.

The cure for a feeling of defeat is a fresh encounter with God.

Get alone with Him, and you'll experience what Daman is talking about when he wrote, "The awareness of what God has called us to do for Him is the basis for overcoming discouragement."

Lack of pride in the assignment God has given will defeat pastor and people. Daman quotes a very strong but clear and true statement from David Ray:

> Low self-esteem is a cancer that kills small churches. It reduces the amount of available money, results in poor building upkeep, repels new members, discourages leaders, erodes organizational effectiveness, changes communication from positive to negative, causes church fights, undermines planning, and limits relationships with those outside. In short, it undermines the ministry and mission of the church. Efforts to enhance personal and church self-esteem need to top a small church's priority list (221).

Again, I urge you to take pride in the assignment God has given to you. You're blessed to be trusted by God with some of the people for whom Jesus died. What a compliment! He may not have called you to a major assignment, but neither did He call Andrew, Peter's brother.

Andrew never wrote a book, was left out of the inner circle, and as far as we know never preached a sermon. He lived in the shadow of his brother, Simon Peter. Should he have been discouraged and defeated? I don't think so! He successfully carried out his role, which was simply to be an "introducer." Because he followed that role, Simon followed Jesus, a multitude was fed, and some Greeks met the Master as He rode into Jerusalem the final week of His life.

Andrew was never in the spotlight, and we don't think of Him first when we think of disciples. We think of Peter, James, and John (the megachurch pastors of that day). However, surely God was pleased with Andrew's faithfulness. Who knows how many people will be in heaven because of his obedience to his call?

Each one of us has a role to fulfill in the Kingdom. We may

never be in the inner circle of megachurches, but if we're faithful, our Father will be pleased and proud of us.

Therefore, we should take pride in the fact that we have given our Heavenly Father our best.

One of the great authors and pastors of our day, Charles Swindoll, beautifully speaks to the importance of our attitudes. The first time I saw this, I was in the office of my cardiologist. You won't be surprised when I tell you that I'm glad my heart doctor takes pride in his attitude.

ATTITUDES

Words can never adequately convey the incredible impact of our attitude toward life. The longer I live the more convinced I become that life is 10 percent what happens to us and 90 percent how we respond to it.

I believe the single most significant decision I can make on a day-to-day basis is my choice of attitude. It is more important than my past, my education, my bankroll, my successes or failures, fame or pain, what other people think of me or say about me, my circumstances, or my position. Attitude keeps me going or cripples my progress. It alone fuels my fire or assaults my hope. When my attitudes are right, there's no barrier too high, no valley too deep, no dream too extreme, no challenge too great for me.*

POINTS TO PONDER

1. Consider: There are no small assignments in God's kingdom. What does this say to you?
2. The key to experiencing pride in our assignment is to clearly understand why we do what we do. Are you experiencing this in your ministry?

*Charles R. Swindoll. *Strengthening Your Grip* (Nashville, Tenn.: W. Publishing Group, 1982), 206-7. Used by permission of Charles R. Swindoll, Inc.

3. How much pride do you take in the assignment God has given you? Carefully consider that "every pastor is the carrier of an attitude."

4. What attitude are you passing on to your congregation?

Scripture

Each one should test his own actions. Then he can take pride in himself without comparing himself to somebody else (Gal. 6:4).

Prayer

Dear Father, I recognize the blessing You've bestowed upon me by calling me into the ministry. Help me to serve You so well that I can take pride in what I'm doing. May I be a carrier of a positive attitude toward the joy Your will provides in my life. In Jesus' name I pray. Amen.

7
POWER

**There is power available in the
shadow of the steeple.**

In his early days some of the neighborhood kids called him "runt." However, no one ever questioned his quickness or athletic ability. They just had trouble believing that he would ever be big enough to play football in a way that would make a difference.

They have long since quit wondering. His heart made up for what he lacked in size, and this year Barry Sanders was inducted into the NFL Football Hall of Fame at Canton, Ohio. At North High School in Wichita, Kansas, he was considered too small to be a starter at the beginning of the year. But once he got a chance to play, his size never got in his way. He not only was a star running back in high school but also went on to Oklahoma State University, where he was an All-American and the winner of the Heisman Trophy as the Outstanding College Football Player in the nation.

From there he went on to be one of the most successful running backs in the history of the National Football League (NFL). Barry Sanders decided to retire just short of the all-time rushing record of Walter Peyton, who had been considered one of the greatest football players of all time.

Did this happen because he grew and became huge? No! It was because he had a desire to make the most of what he had. Most NFL running backs are big and fast. Barry never weighed much more than 200 pounds. He was always small and quick, but he was also extremely strong. More than anything, he had heart. He had a desire to excel, so he made up in strength for what he lacked in size. This is the key issue to success in any field, and I believe it's especially true in the field of church ministry.

Success did not come easy for Barry. He worked long and hard at strengthening his abilities. Convenience and comfort never got in his way. One of my sons, Pat, worked out some with him at the Wichita State University football stadium. After running multiple laps around the field and many wind sprints and passing routes, Pat was exhausted and ready to go home. Not Barry! He would have Pat or one of the other guys climb onto his back. Then he would run up the stadium steps again and again. This enabled him to develop great strength to go along with the quickness that was in his legs. Why did he work so hard? His heart for football would not let his size keep him from excelling. The power was there. He just had to train it so that it could be used for his purposes.

You don't have to be a megachurch to make a difference in your community.

A person can only wonder what impact small churches could make for the Kingdom if they would simply harvest the power that's available. It's not easy. However, if the pastor and church members have the heart to make the most of the potential God has given to them, they can do something significant for His kingdom. You don't have to be a megachurch to make a difference in your community.

If desire can motivate a football player to develop all his potential, how can the church be satisfied to be "quick" but too small to make a difference? Why should the church let size (or the lack of it) defeat them when the power to excel is available?

There's no place for weak, heartless congregations. But

there is a significant role for strong, small churches even if they're located in the shadow of a megachurch steeple.

Barry Sanders would be the first one to point out that his success was enhanced by the huge linemen on his team. He was always expressing his gratitude for their efforts. So it is with the church. Let the "huge church" open the holes through which the small strong church can run.

While some people automatically connect "small" with "weak," that is a mistake. Not all small churches are weak, just as not all small people are weak. As I've endeavored to illustrate, some small people have great strengths that can be developed and used for success in their chosen fields of activity.

Power is available to any church regardless of its size. The key to making the most of its potential is to tap into that resource. And what is that resource? It's God's power. Again, I turn to Kennon Callahan: "Our promise is in the possibilities God gives to us. The strengths we have are God's gift to us. God invites us to grow stronger, not bigger. God encourages us to build on the strength with which God blesses us. God wants for us a strong promising presence" (*Small, Strong Congregations*, 300). Please note this statement: "God invites us to grow stronger, not bigger." This runs counter to the popular concept of the modern Church world. However, it's very compatible with the New Testament mandate as set forth in the Book of Acts.

The Early Church began with a small band of dedicated believers. Jesus did not promise them size. He promised them power. We read in Acts 1:8, "You will receive power when the Holy Spirit comes upon you; and you will be my witnesses in Jerusalem, and in all Judea and Samaria, and to the ends of the earth." The promise is clear—power. And the promise is still clear today—power to carry out our assignment to be witnesses to our world is still available, and that Power will enable us to make a difference.

When the small strong church in Jerusalem tapped into the

Vision is the key to tapping into the source of power that God has available for carrying out the desire He has placed with each of us.

power supply Jesus promised, they changed their community. So can we today. We may not reach thousands, as the church in Jerusalem did, but we can have a life-changing effect on our community. What we accomplish for God will be determined by the size of our heart for the work rather than the size of our building. *If you have a heart for His work, God has the power available for you to accomplish it.*

In *Beyond the Ordinary* Woolever and Bruce quote Lance Secretan: "Leadership is not so much about technique and methods as it is about opening the heart. Leadership is about inspiration" (93). Inspiration to do what? To tap into the power source that God has made available. Techniques and methods are important and will be helpful in carrying out our assignments. But power is the critical factor.

Power is to the church what fuel is to an automobile. It does not matter very much the size of the automobile or the gadgets that it may have if there's no fuel in the tank. It's the fuel that enables the automobile to carry out its assignment of transporting passengers to their chosen destination. A small car "with power" may not carry as many as the limousine, but it can carry some who otherwise would not have a ride. Power is readily available to enable the small vehicle to fulfill its purpose just as well as the luxury limo.

So it is with the church. A small church will not carry as many members as the megachurch. But it will take people to the foot of the Cross who would not have made it otherwise. So rather than being defeated because of what they don't have in the way of equipment, resources, and programs, pastors of small churches should be excited about the power that's readily available to them. And they should excite their people with the possibilities of fulfilling the assignments God has given them.

Woolever and Bruce are clear in their statement: "What congregations accomplish or fail to achieve is more often controlled by their vision of what they can do rather than by their internal circumstance or their community context" (102). In other words, congregations are more controlled by vision than by any other factor. Vision, then, is the key to tapping into the source of power that God has available for carrying out the desire He has placed with each of us.

Do smaller churches ever tap into the power supply available to them? Apparently some do. In fact, according to the Scriptures, the pattern of grasping the power God has available has not changed. Some churches have a vision of what He wants them to do and commit themselves to that. The church at Philadelphia, addressed in Rev. 3:7-13, is a great illustration of this.

Many scholars believe the words "I know that you have little strength" (v. 8) refer to the size of the church rather than their spiritual strength. In fact, some believe that this church was hardly visible in the community and that the people were drawn from the poorer classes. This would certainly qualify the Philadelphian congregation as a small church located in the shadow of larger, more visible churches.

Philadelphia did not begin to compare in size and importance with Ephesus, which was the leading city in the Roman province in Asia. It's safe to assume that the churches in those two cities would have experienced some of the same contrasts. We can safely assume that at one time the church in Ephesus was considerably stronger than the one in Philadelphia and would have overshadowed that tiny church. According to Acts 20:31, Paul, the greatest voice of his day, spent nearly three years in Ephesus. He won many converts, both Jews and Gentiles, and built a strong church. Timothy was there for a while, and Early Church tradition shows that John the beloved apostle spent the last years of his life at this great center of believers.

Surely the church at Philadelphia could never be as pleasing to God as the church at Ephesus. They were small and insignificant in the world of their day. The reality is that they *were* more pleasing to God than the church at Ephesus. Look at God's message to Ephesus in Rev. 2:3-5— "You have persevered and have endured hardships for my name, and have not grown weary. Yet I hold this against you: You have forsaken your first love. Remember the height from which you have fallen!" God was not pleased with that big, important church of the first century.

Now look at His words to the small church at Philadelphia in Rev. 3:8-10—"I know your deeds. See, I have placed before you an open door that no one can shut. I know you have little strength. Yet you have kept my word. . . . Since you have kept my command to endure patiently, I will also keep you from the hour of trial that is going to come upon the whole world."

God is pleased with a small, strong faithful church. How did that church maintain its strength in a hostile world? The people took advantage of the power God made available to them. Note verse 8: "You have kept my word and have not denied my name." In other words, they found strength in the Word to carry out their assignment. Being too small to make a visible impact on their city did not prevent them from being faithful. Without the deep financial pockets that were accessible to some other churches of their day, they were still able to please God.

The church at Philadelphia had a vision to be God's voice to the many merchants who passed through their city on their way to the spice markets in the eastern Mediterranean world. It was that vision that tapped into God's resources. And those resources are always more than adequate for God's church to carry out its assignment.

One of my favorite stories in the Bible is that of the feeding of the 5,000 as recorded in John 6. Every time I read this story, I'm prodded to note that it was the smallest, most unlikely person in the crowd whom Jesus chose to use for His glory.

When we make available to God what we have, we tap into His power.

We would think that either Peter, James, or John, the big steeple guys, would have been the one Jesus would have used. After all, they were the most visible and outspoken ones in the crowd. But Jesus taught a marvelous lesson when He used what an unnamed little boy had to offer. We still don't know his name, and he still exists in the shadow of the big three. However, on that day that little lad's willingness to place what he had at Jesus' disposal enabled him to be a conductor of God's power to a vast multitude of people.

The key lesson in this miracle is that anyone can be used of God for His purposes regardless of how insignificant he or she might seem from the world's perspective. When we make available to Him what we have, we tap into His power.

Smaller churches ministering in the shadow of larger, much more visible churches have a very vital role in the Kingdom. Willingness to make available whatever we have taps into God's power, and wonderful things happen as a result.

It was just such a church that God used to change the life of one of the most popular women on today's Christian circuit. Becky Tirabassi speaks to hundreds of thousands around the world each year. But the launching of her impact began with an encounter with God in a small church that had tapped into God's power source. She described that encounter in her book *Let Prayer Change Your Life:*

I often shake my head in awe at the miracle of my conversion to Christ. For six years, from the ages of fifteen to twenty-one, I followed all the "popular" trends: going to wild parties, drinking, dancing, bar hopping and using drugs. . . .

An unusual course of events led me to a small church with one born-again, Spirit-filled janitor on its staff who loved to share the person of Christ with the lost. Never, in my wildest thoughts, would I have imagined my life turning 180 degrees one hot, sunny, August California afternoon at the persuasion of this janitor.

How did he convince me to be born again when my boyfriend, lifestyle, and future looked so worldly? He spoke these words: "If anyone is in Christ, he is a new creation; old things have passed away; behold, all things have become new" (2 Corinthians 5:17, NKJV).

And though this janitor knew of my past and present, he told me that Jesus loved me—just the way I was! . . .

. . . I was without hope for healing, no money for even outpatient recovery. I had literally depleted any reservoir of self-respect. What could cause such a turnaround?

I believe the first step of faith took place when I believed what the janitor said about His Jesus: (1) He did and would always love me, and (2) He was going to make my life new.

The second step occurred when I repeated the "sinner's prayer," begged Jesus to come into my heart and forgive me of my many sins and make me new. I walked away from that time in prayer convinced that I was a brand-new person! (138-39).

That small, strong church had hooked onto God's power supply. The custodian reflected the vision of the church, to reach lost people with the message of Jesus. I don't know the name of the church or the janitor, but I can guarantee you—God does! And that's what really matters.

Only eternity will reveal the joy that has come as the result of a small church in California that abides in the shadow of some tall, highly visible steeples—a small church that dared to tap into God's divine power.

If it were possible for you to visit with NFL All-Pro Barry Sanders personally, I guarantee you that he would make it clear—that *you do not have to be big to be strong and successful in your assignment.*

POINTS TO PONDER

1. There's a significant role for strong, small churches even when they're located in the shadow of a megachurch steeple. What does this statement mean to you?
2. Have you realized "More people will be drawn to the small, strong congregation than any other kind of congregation"? What does this statement mean to you?
3. Think about this: The Early Church began with a small band of dedicated believers. Jesus did not promise them size. How does this relate to your church?
4. Since what congregations accomplish or fail to accomplish is controlled by their vision, what should a pastor spend a major portion of his or her energy doing?

Scripture

With great power the apostles continued to testify to the resurrection of the Lord Jesus, and much grace was upon them all (Acts 4:33).

Prayer

Dear Father, give me the power I need for the opportunity You've set before me. May I take my eyes from the smallness of the church I pastor and fix them on the greatness of Your blessing. In Christ's name I pray. Amen.

8
PROVISION

There is provision in the shadow of the steeple.

"Sister Williams, what's wrong over there?" With that question and a series of subsequent actions by godly people, I learned in a very powerful way that God provides for us to carry out His will. I was pastoring a baby church in the shadow of some strong, mature congregations.

I had called home earlier to tell my first wife, Bettye, that I would be home for lunch. She responded, "There's no reason to come unless you have some money to buy food on the way home. There's nothing here." I thought she was kidding, but she wasn't. I didn't have a dime to my name. We had no credit cards—those were preplastic days—and we didn't even have a checking account. So I couldn't even write a "hot" check and ask the grocer to hold it for a day or two. We were totally broke.

I still thought she was exaggerating. Surely there was something in the pantry, but I soon discovered that there was absolutely nothing there. Our cupboards were truly bare.

We had three children under six years of age. How could we explain to a six-year-old that it was prayer-and-fasting day? Should I have said, "Just think. You get to go hungry and pray for the other hungry children in the world." I wasn't looking forward to that. Bettye and I would be OK. But I must confess that I was concerned about the kids. It was Wednesday, and I would get my $50 weekly salary at church that night. We could get food on our way home from church. But that was nine hours away, and all three of our children would really be hungry by then.

I began to look for pop bottles throughout and under our little prefabricated house that sat on concrete blocks. Then I searched the neighborhood. At that time bottles could be redeemed for two cents each. I found enough empty bottles to buy a can of tomato soup, a package of Kool-Aid, and a tube of crackers. At least the kids could have something for lunch. Bettye mixed the soup with water and got lunch ready for the kids.

Just as they finished saying grace, the phone rang. It was Mrs. Adams, one of our 12 members, calling to inquire about our situation. Before we knew we had a problem, God had been working on providing for us. After Mrs. Adams asked what was wrong, she went on to explain that throughout the morning her heart had been heavy. God had kept directing her thoughts to our little family in the church parsonage.

What God calls us to do, He provides for us to do. When we pursue His will, we travel on His resources.

Bettye explained the problem but went on to tell Mrs. Adams that we would be all right. She told her that I would get my check that night and would buy some food on the way home from church. "Don't worry about us—everything will be all right," Bettye said.

Mrs. Adams didn't press the issue. However, she got on the phone and called some of the Christians she knew in the established churches in the area. Before supper that evening, they pulled up before our house in a station wagon crammed with food. They even cooked a chicken and had other food so that we could have a hot meal that evening before church. We were blessed to be near some true believers.

As I mentioned earlier, our little church was a brand-new plant in the shadow of some strong congregations. We had no financial strength. A sponsoring board had promised to give us $50 each week for 90 days. After that, they said, "You'll be on your own."

Not true! We were never truly on our own. *What God calls us to do, He provides for us to do. When we pursue His will, we travel on His resources.* He had led me to leave an established church and move into that location to plant a baby church. From the moment we responded to His call, He knew of our need long before it happened.

He also knew that the experience of His provision would be so firmly implanted in my mind that I would lose all fear of ever being in need.

It was that experience that provided an entrée into our community. I knew I would need to find additional income in order to support my family. So I went to the local high school to see if there were any openings. To my amazement, they hired me to teach English and to coach football and basketball. This opened all kinds of doors and contacts for our little church. The students in my classes and the boys on my teams were responsive to the church.

It was a "God-thing" that I was able to teach. You see, as I had studied and worked my way through college, He had directed my curriculum choices. I did not deliberately choose classes that would qualify me to be a public school teacher. That possibility had never crossed my mind. However, when I sent in my transcripts, I met all the requirements for teaching in the state of Florida. My Divine Guidance Counselor had very quietly provided for needs that were still five to ten years in the future.

I don't believe I was a special case. In fact, as I've shared that story across the country time after time, others have shared similar experiences with me. These are great moments that people who have never had "close calls" can't enjoy.

Once we learn firsthand that God does indeed provide for

us to carry out His assignment—whatever that might be—we lose all fear of the unknown. The Bible is full of times when God provided for his special servants in a special way so that they could carry out their assignments. And don't lose sight of the fact that pastoring a small church in the shadow of the steeple is a special assignment. Pastors of such churches have been examined by God and found to be capable of carrying out this special task.

Small-church pastors must have
- Total commitment to God's will
- Absolute faith in God's Word
- The ability to work without recognition
- A willingness to work hard
- A strong awareness of God's assignment
- A naïveté that believes God's revealed will is the best thing that could happen in their lives at any particular time

Notice that I did not say that they could find comfort. Moses was not comfortable in Exod. 3:10, when God told him, "I am sending you to Pharaoh to bring my people, the Israelites, out of Egypt." Moses kept "negotiating" with God because he felt inadequate to face the challenge. In fact, in Exod. 4:10 Moses said, "O Lord, I have never been eloquent, neither in the past nor since you have spoken to your servant. I am slow of speech and tongue."

Since Moses would be negotiating the release of the Israelites from Egypt, we would think it would be advantageous for him to be able to speak fluently. Yet he recognized and acknowledged his weakness.

No problem! God provided Aaron to be Moses' spokesman. He said, "I will help both of you speak and will teach you what to do" (Exod. 4:15). In other words, *Trust Me, Moses. I'll provide for you to carry out My will.* Moses had God's promise that what He had called him to do (lead the children of Israel out of Egypt), He would provide the wisdom, strength, and will for him to do.

That promise of provision is extended to every pastor, and I believe it's especially appropriate for all small-church pastors. God extends the promise of His presence, provision, and anything else that's needed to carry out His will. Many small-church pastors are so absorbed in survival that they often miss the feeling of confidence that God wants them to enjoy.

In his book *Small Strong Congregations,* Kennon Callahan writes,

> God wants us to live with promise. We look for some promise in life. Then . . . God's promise is that amid all the problems and possibilities of living, God is with us—fully, completely. The strength of God's grace, the gentleness of God's compassion, the encouragement of God's hope sees us forward. We live with confidence and assurance because of the promise of God (291).

We live with confidence and assurance because of the promise of God. And what is that promise? That He will provide everything we need to carry out His will. He always has, and His program has not changed.

Do yourself a favor. Take hold of God's promise to provide everything you need to fulfill His will. Enjoy the confidence He holds out to you. Make the most of the privilege to be His instrument in reaching people who don't, and probably never will, attend a megachurch.

Many small-church pastors are so absorbed in survival that they often miss the feeling of confidence that God wants them to enjoy.

It always excites me to see how God provides for the needs of small churches. And His provision happens in so many different ways.

- A small church in our city did not have a worship leader. The pastor had left secular employment to shepherd the very small flock that worshiped in the very midst of some tall steeples. He needed help, so God provided it. He inspired the best soloist in town to leave the large church she was attending to worship with that tiny congregation. It wasn't long before she began to lead worship, and the need that had existed was more than adequately supplied.

- Severy, Kansas, is not exactly in the shadow of a big church steeple. In fact, it's about 50 miles out in the country. However, God used a large church in Wichita to provide for the needs of that small church. The pastor at Severy was invited to come to a Sunday School class Christmas party at the large church. On that trip his car "gave up the ghost." He needed help. God laid that need on the heart of the large-church pastor. With the help of some dedicated laypersons, God provided wheels for that young pastor and his family.

- The Church of the Nazarene in Sebring, Florida, was averaging about 45 in attendance when I became their pastor. I attended a camp meeting where I felt led to explain to the speaker and singer that I would love to have them come to our church at some point, but we could not afford them. I'll never forget their response. They said, "We'll come for anything or nothing." When I told the church that some of the country's greatest evangelists and singers were coming to our church, their faces lit up. God had provided a major spiritual boost for a small church.

I could go on and on about situations of which I'm personally aware in which God has intervened so that His will could be accomplished. Yes, I know that there are a lot of struggling churches, and I don't know why nothing good seems to be happening in some of them. However, I don't believe that God wants things to remain like that. I'm convinced that He fully intends to provide whatever is needed to fulfill His will.

One of the major battles small-church pastors face is a feeling of inadequacy and hopelessness. Satan robs them of their self-respect because the church is tiny and not much appears to be happening. Those pastors should be excited, because at any moment God could do something special.

E. V. Hill in his book *A Savior Worth Having* offers encouragement for all of us. He writes,

> When you have Jesus, you become subject to receive at any moment, fantastic, unbelievable, divine supplement. Nobody is sufficient within himself. All of us come to a point when we can just get so far and no further. We all need somebody who is able to put a little rope on the end of our grasp. You can't do it yourself. You need somebody to reach out to help you, and you don't deserve it. And it's not a result of whether or not you prayed all night or whether or not you have more faith than someone else. It doesn't mean He loves you more. It means that every now and then in God's own sovereign will He says, "Here." He is able to do it. And He does it because every now and then you need help (110).

So what do you need that God does not have in abundant supply? Why would He withhold help from you when you're pursuing His will? That's right. He has an abundance of everything and fully intends to make provision for you to carry out the assignment with which He has entrusted you.

You may not understand why you're being asked to carry out an assignment that's difficult. Neither did Abraham in Gen. 22, when God instructed him to take Isaac up the mountain and offer him as a sacrifice.

Looking at the decision facing this man of God, we would naturally think that it seemed too much to ask. How could God ask Abraham to give up this precious son for whom he and Sarah had prayed for years? This was the son of their old age, and Isaac had brought great joy to them. Now God was asking for Isaac to be offered as a sacrifice. Abraham had been faithful and obedient. Why this test?

Who can ever say why God does what He does or why He asks us to do certain things? We don't know what He knows or see the future that only He can see. Years ago, when He led me to leave an established church in Sebring, Florida, to plant a new church in Gainesville, Florida, no one understood the move. In fact, the leading pastor in Sebring was very blunt: "Gene, to take Bettye and those babies and move to Gainesville is crazy. It makes no sense." Neither Bettye nor I knew what God had planned. But we eventually discovered that He had planned a future that would grow out of that move that was beyond our wildest dreams.

So when God asks for the unusual, wise people respond. As Abraham and Isaac went up the mountain, Isaac asked, "Father? . . . The fire and the wood are here . . . but where is the lamb for the burnt offering?" (Gen. 22:7). I have an idea that Abraham's heart was heavy, but his faith in God was like flint. He responded, "God himself will provide the lamb for the burnt offering, my son" (v. 8)

What Abraham did not know was that as he and Isaac were climbing one side of the mountain, God had a ram coming up the other side. They met at the site where the sacrifice was to be offered. God had provided! And He still makes provision for our needs today.

We don't understand why God asks us to do the things He requires of us. We're not called to understand—we're called to be faithful. Any pastor who will be obedient and keep the faith even when it seems too much to ask will truly discover that God still provides today.

I can tell you from firsthand encounters that experiencing

the providing grace of God is exciting and liberating. When we know you're where God wants you to be, you may be uncomfortable at times, but you lose your fear of the situation in which you find yourself because of God's faithfulness in the past. Nothing confirms our faith like a memory walk back to His provision in our yesterdays.

Don't be surprised if when you find yourself climbing various mountains of service wondering how you can survive that particular trial, you hear a voice within saying, "Press on up the mountain." Then, sure enough, when you come to the critical moment, God will always have a ram ready to meet your need.

POINTS TO PONDER

1. Consider: What God calls us to do, He enables us to do. How does this relate to you?
2. Have you realized the comfort and assurance that come because the promises of God are worthy of trust? Do you fully trust Him?
3. What mountain of difficulty are you currently climbing? What's coming up the other side of the mountain?
4. Consider seriously: What do you need that God can't provide?

Scripture

My God will meet all your needs according to his glorious riches in Christ Jesus (Phil. 4:19).

Prayer

Dear Father, thank You for opening the doors to Your great storehouse to me. I realize that You have more of anything I'll ever need than I can imagine. You've already been overly gracious in Your blessings. Thank You. Help me to face my call in absolute confidence that You'll provide everything I need.

9
PEACE

There is peace in the shadow of the steeple.

"'I know the plans I have for you,' declares the LORD, 'plans to prosper you and not to harm you, plans to give you hope and a future'" (Jer. 29:11).

Where you are and what's happening in your life is not surprising to God. It may be surprising to you, but He has always known just where you would be right now. Since everything that comes into our lives is first filtered through the love of God, we should be at peace with His will. Please notice that I did not say you would always be comfortable. I said, "at peace." You can truly experience peace regardless of your circumstances because your Father has wonderful plans for you, and He believes in you. He knows you can be a successful vessel right where He has assigned you to serve.

He did send you there, didn't He? I mean, before you accepted the call to your present assignment, you did talk to Him about it, didn't you? So you're there by divine appointment. *Remember—He does not have plans to harm you but "to give you hope and a future"* (Jer. 29:11).

In order to experience peace, we must determine that we are indeed under divine appointment. I have strong confidence in Prov. 3:5-6: "Trust in the LORD with all your heart and lean not on your own understanding; in all your ways acknowledge him, and he will make your paths straight."

Because of that promise (which I have embraced with absolute confidence), I've experienced a deep sense of inner peace even during the times in my life when the waters around me were greatly troubled.

We have peace because the One who overcame the worst conditions in the world loves us and has great plans that have not yet been fulfilled.

You can be sure that Satan does not want you to communicate a sense of positive joy to your people. To do so would encourage their faith. The enemy wants to keep you and your people discouraged. However, you can experience the promise of Jesus in John 16:33—"I have told you these things so that in me you may have peace. In this world you will have trouble. But take heart! I have overcome the world." If you adopt that promise as your own, you'll be able to maintain a positive attitude toward all of life.

Numbers never produce peace. It's nice when they look good, but you'll *always* want more people in your congregation. Financial strength can't produce peace. It's nice to be able to pay the bills, but more will always be on the way. Not even the love of your people will give you peace. These things certainly are nice, and it's wonderful when they're in the positive column. However, deep inner peace comes from knowing who has the final say in all circumstances concerning your life. We have peace because the One who overcame the worst conditions in the world loves us and has great plans that have not yet been fulfilled. We find great comfort in Isa. 26:3—"You will keep in perfect peace him whose mind is steadfast, because he trusts in you."

In his book *The Practice of Godliness* Jerry Bridges has a beautiful chapter on joy. He deals with the source of joy when he points out that Jesus cautioned against making the basis of our joy the fact that we're successful in ministry. He then goes on to write, "Success in ministry comes and goes, but our names are written in heaven forever" (136).

I would like to edit that statement to point out that peace, a true inner peace, should not—must not—be based on success in ministry. When peace is based on what's happening positively in ministry, then it will come and go like the waves of the sea. When our peace is founded firmly on God's faithfulness, it's a deep, lasting peace. Success is wonderful when it happens, and we should certainly work faithfully to that end. *But peace is the result of being where I know God wants me to be and doing what I know He wants me to do.* And there needs to be no question about our assignment. He led you to your present assignment so that Jesus, the hope of all humanity, would be lifted up. He never leaves anyone who is being obedient to His leadership to his or her own ability.

Look at Peter in Matt. 14:22-33. Jesus invited him to walk on top of the stormy waters of the Sea of Galilee. He was safe until he took his eyes off Jesus. Still, when he turned his eyes back to the One who had instructed him to get out of the boat, he was once again able to walk on the water back to the boat. Peter could do what Jesus instructed him to do. And so can you! Remember—He instructed you to take the responsibility to pastor that church, and He intends to honor your obedience.

We could look at multiple situations in which obedience produced wonderful results, but let's look at one more instance. In John 5 we meet a man who was frustrated by his situation. It seemed hopeless, and according to verse 7 he had struggled for years with a condition beyond his control. "I have no one to help me into the pool when the water is stirred. While I am trying to get in, someone else goes down ahead of me" (v. 7).

There were times in the early years of pastoring when I felt that I had "no one to help me." I led the singing, taught a Sunday School class, opened and closed the church building. You get the idea. It was physically exhausting, and there were many times when I wondered where I could find some help. It would have been defeating except for the deep inner peace that came from the One who said, *I'll help you.* In my first five assignments as a pastor I had "no one but Jesus" to help me do what I needed to do for Him. But I had *Him.* I frequently heard Him say, *I'll help you. I really will. Just trust Me.* Because of that sustaining promise, I experienced great peace. After all, He was the one I most wanted to please.

In his classic book *Peace with God*, Billy Graham speaks to the two great experiences of peace that believers (pastors, too) can enjoy. First, he writes about peace *with* God. You're in the ministry because somewhere in your life you came to Jesus and realized you could be at peace with God by the grace of Christ. Second, Dr. Graham speaks to the great offer of the peace *of* God (270-71):

> Everyone who knows the Lord Jesus Christ can go through any problem, and face death, and still have the peace of God in his heart. When your spouse dies, or your children get sick, or you lose your job, you can have a peace that you don't understand. You may have tears at a graveside, but you can have an abiding peace, a quietness. . . .
>
> Colossians 3:15 says, "Let the peace of God rule in your hearts." Some of you believe that you know Jesus Christ as your Savior, but you haven't really made Him your Lord. You are missing the peace of God in your struggles and turmoils and trials and pressures of life. Is the peace of God in your heart? . . .
>
> There is no human philosophy that achieves such changes or provides such strength. This mighty strength stands ready to be available at your beck and call at all times. God said, "Fear thou not; For I am with thee: Be not dismayed; For I am thy God: I will strengthen thee; Yea, I

will help thee; Yea, I will uphold thee with the right hand of my righteousness" (Isaiah 41:10).

Whatever the circumstances, whatever the call, whatever the duty, whatever the price, whatever the sacrifice—His strength will be your strength in your hour of need.

I love that last statement: *"His* strength will be *your* strength in your hour of need" (emphasis added). This promise is the foundation for the peace that every pastor can experience regardless of the size of the steeple on his or her church. And you can have this peace even if you don't have a steeple.

In the Introduction I mentioned the fact that many pastors are struggling because their church does not even reach midlevel (which is 200-300) in attendance. They feel discouraged because they're reaching only 35-60 attendees on the average Sunday. And when they think of the glamorous megachurch situations, they really struggle. Add to that the televangelists whose super-slick services are piped into the homes of their people via television, and many pastors wonder, *Why try? I can't compete with them. My people wonder why we struggle to have a piano player when television brings a symphonic orchestra right into their living rooms. They say, "Why don't we just stay home and worship with the gifted television crowd? Or if we are going to make the effort to go to church, why shouldn't we go to the huge church with their great, multifaceted program?"*

Before you let the glamour of the television church and the power of the megachurch intimidate you, remember why you're pastoring where you are. God sent you there. He believes in you. He has some people there who will never attend the huge churches or know His forgiveness and love by simply sitting at home and watching the preacher on television. *God loves them so much that He sent you as an ambassador of His love and grace.*

God may not expect you to reach a multitude. It may be that you're to minister to just one. But if that's what He has assigned you to do, you can find great peace and joy in winning just one.

Remember the story that Jesus told in Luke 15 about the shepherd who had one sheep outside the fold. There was only one lost sheep out of 99. Still, the shepherd was not satisfied until the last sheep was found and brought safely back into the fold. "Then he calls his friends and neighbors together and says, 'Rejoice with me; I have found my lost sheep'" (v. 6). One found sheep was the cause for a celebration and brought great joy to the heart of the shepherd.

God has sent you to reach those separated from the multitude. He is pleased with your "one." If you're listening, you'll hear Him say, "Well done, faithful servant." To know that you've brought joy to the heart of God should bring peace to your heart.

There's peace in the shadow of the steeple of a megachurch or in the glow of a glamorous television service. In fact, those pastors who are faithfully and obediently serving where God has assigned them can experience a deep, abiding peace. Years ago, Frances de Sales wrote the lines I want to use as an encouragement to you as I close this work. May God bless the anonymous person who preserved and passed on these wonderful words.

God may not expect you to reach a multitude. It may be that you're to minister to just one.

BE AT PEACE
Francis de Sales

Do not look forward to what may happen tomorrow.
The same everlasting Father Who cares for you today
Will care for you tomorrow and every day.
Either He will shield you from suffering

Or He will give you unfailing strength to bear it.
Be at peace, then.
Put aside all anxious thoughts and imaginations
And say continuously,
"The Lord is my strength and shield.
My heart has trusted in Him,
He has forgiven me, and I am helped.
He is not only with me but in me,
And I am in Him."
If this is true in your life, then—be at peace!

POINTS TO PONDER

1. Since God has plans for you, as He promised in Jer. 29:11, what does that mean to you in your present assignment?
2. If an obedient Peter could walk on top of storm water, so can you. Think about that.
3. Are you experiencing the peace of God of which Billy Graham wrote?
1. Seriously consider: If God sent you on an assignment to win "one," what should your response be to that challenge?

Scripture

Peace I leave with you; my peace I give you. I do not give to you as the world gives. Do not let your hearts be troubled and do not be afraid (John 14:27).

Prayer

Dear Father, Thank You for loving me and believing in me. I'm grateful for the assignment You have entrusted into my keeping. Help me to be at peace with Your plans, Your will. I want to be at my very best for You. In Jesus' precious name I pray. Amen.

EPILOGUE

I sat on the platform of one of the churches I pastored, looked out at the congregation, and all but said out loud, *This is too hard to face. Why must I go through this? Surely I don't have to face such situations.*

I didn't need to express my feelings out loud. *He* heard me. Before I could wallow deeper into my "pity party," God said, *Look at the Cross. Just for your information, that was not an easy experience either.* I can honestly say that on that day I turned a corner in my attitude toward any assignment God would ever give me. The Lord believed in me enough to put me in that place at that time. He entrusted me with the spiritual care of some people for whom He had died.

Remember the compliment God has given to you. He did call you to your church, didn't He? He believes you're the shepherd that group of people needs at this particular time. He has committed himself to help you make the most of this opportunity to care for His sheep. What a compliment!

So the next time you, like me, begin to wonder why and let the situation in which you find yourself let you down, read the words to this old song, and let them speak to your heart.

LITTLE IS MUCH WHEN GOD IS IN IT

In the harvest field now ripened
There's a work for all to do;
Hark! the voice of God is calling
To the harvest calling you.

Does the place you're called to labor
Seem so small and little known?
It is great if God is in it,
And He'll not forget His own.

. . . .

When the conflict here is ended
And our race on earth is run,
He will say, if we are faithful,
"Welcome home, My child—well done!"

Little is much when God is in it!
Labor not for wealth or fame.
There's a crown—and you can win it,
If you go in Jesus' name.
                —Kittie L. Suffield

1202261

250
W7233

LINCOLN CHRISTIAN UNIVERSITY

126864

250 W7233
Williams, Gene, 1932-
In the shadow of the steeple

3 4711 00217 4490